Pass the Port

The best after-dinner stories of the famous

Pass the Port

The best after-dinner stories of the famous

Christian Brann
Cirencester

ISBN 0 9504923 1 0

Published to advance the work of

The stories in this book
were generously donated
by their famous contributors
to Oxfam, to whom all
royalties will be given.

First published 1976
Revised edition 1978
Second revised edition 1979
Third edition 1981
Fourth revised edition 1982
Reprinted 1984

This book was devised, published and printed by
Christian Brann Limited, Cirencester.
Illustrations by Brian Blake.

Introduction

Laughter in the face of adversity is not the sole prerogative of the British, although we are renowned for it and it has made many of the darker periods of our history bearable.

The main objectives of Oxfam are to fight hunger and adversity in those parts of the world where even the basic necessities of life are still in short supply. A book of after-dinner stories may appear to be far removed from these objectives and yet the generous donors of the stories contained in this book — many of them famous names with a distinguished record of service around the world — have contributed more than money to the cause of Oxfam.

Stories from the personal experience of such eminent men as Prince Philip, the Duke of Edinburgh, the Archbishop of Canterbury, Denis Healey, J.B. Priestley and hundreds of others, form a unique collection which is bound to attract many thousands of readers. Because all the royalties and publishing profits of this book have been donated to Oxfam, it will not only bring laughter and enjoyment to its readers but every copy sold will help the work of Oxfam. We hope that those who enjoy the book will make a present of it to others and will encourage their friends to buy it too.

It has often been said that laughter is a cure for all manner of ills. This book will also help to relieve hunger and hardship.

Brian W. Walker
Director
Oxfam
274 Banbury Road
Oxford

Summer 1976

BUCKINGHAM PALACE

A speaker once proposed a toast to my health in terms rather more generous than usual and to cap it all quoted these two lines from John Dryden:-

"A man so various that he seemed to be
Not one but all mankind's epitome."

Fortunately I had seen a draft of his speech before he made it and I was able to look up the quotation before replying. So in responding to the toast I was able to say:-

"Some people might well feel that he has succeeded in presenting me not just in a good light but in a positively rosy glow of perfection. I can only imagine that he has taken Disraeli's advice that 'Everyone likes flattery; and when you come to Royalty you should lay it on with a trowel'. At any rate I hope that what he has left unsaid is not an indication of his true feelings, because the rest of the quotation from Dryden, which he carefully left out, goes like this:-

Stiff in opinions, always in the wrong
Was everything by starts and nothing long;
But in the course of one revolving moon
Was chemist, fiddler, statesman and buffoon."

Philip

Lord Aberconway,
Industrialist; High Sheriff of Denbighshire, 1950.

A psychiatrist, receiving a new patient, observed that she carried under her arm a live duck. However, being accustomed to idiosyncracies he made no comment, and, asking her to be seated, enquired what he could do for her.

"Oh, it's not I who need help, doctor," she replied, "it's my husband here, he thinks he's a duck."

The Late James Smart Abernethy, M.A., LL.B.,
Registrar and Legal Officer, Lands and Surveys Department, Sarawak, 1965-71.

Some years ago two low paid members of the East End Jewish community, having saved up for the purpose, bought themselves a motor car. The day after taking possession of the car they decided to go for a run in the country and set out with Isaac at the wheel. After going some distance they found that they were running short of petrol and driving into a small filling station drew up behind a car filling at the pumps. When this car moved off, the station attendant moved over to the following car.

"Juice?" he asked.

"Vell, vat if ve are?" replied Isaac indignantly, "don't ve get no petrol?"

Lord Abinger, D.L.,
Farmer and Company Director.

Wales was playing England at Rugby football. No bigger or more enthusiastic crowd ever packed the Cardiff ground; the seats had been sold out weeks ahead. But what should Dai Davies see next to his neighbour Mr. Jones, but one empty seat.

"Mr. Jones," he exclaimed, "you have an empty seat beside you."

"Yes," said Mr. Jones, "that seat is Mrs. Jones'."

"But could not Mrs. Jones come to the match?" said Dai.

"No she could not; Mrs. Jones died last week."

"I am sorry," said Dai, "but would not one of your friends have liked Mrs. Jones' seat?"

"No," replied Mr. Jones, "my dear, loyal friends, they are all at Mrs. Jones' funeral today."

The Late Harold Abrahams, C.B.E., M.A., LL.B., Olympic Games Athlete, Author and Broadcaster.

From a schoolboy's essay on Johann Sebastian Bach:

"Johann Sebastian Bach was a most prolific composer. He was the father of twenty children. In his spare time — he practised in the attic on a spinster."

Sir John Ackroyd, Bt., Consultant and Investment Adviser to Middle East Companies.

In his "viva voce" examination for "Divvers" at Oxford, Oscar Wilde was required to translate from the Greek version of the New Testament, which was one of the set books. The passage chosen was from the story of the Passion. Wilde began to translate, easily and accurately. The examiners were satisfied, and told him that this was enough. Wilde ignored them and continued to translate. After another attempt the examiners at last succeeded in stopping him, and told him that they were satisfied with his translation.

"Oh, do let me go on," said Wilde, "I want to see how it ends."

"What's your idea of civilisation?" Bernard Shaw was asked one day.

"It's a good idea," replied Shaw. "Somebody ought to start it."

The Rev. Professor Peter Ackroyd, M.A., Ph.D., D.D., M.Th., Professor of Old Testament Studies, University of London.

Contributed verbatim by my three-year old grandson, Ben Marples:

A little boy ate a lot of buns for his tea. He asked for another, but his father said:

"If you eat another, you'll burst."

"Give me another and stand clear."

Air Vice-Marshal Alexander Adams, C.B., D.F.C.,
Director, The Mental Health Foundation, 1970-77.

It was the end of the Battle of Britain. I had been summoned to a meeting at Fighter Command Headquarters. Approaching Stanmore by car I was stopped by a road sign which said, "Road Closed — Unexploded Bomb". There was a policeman on duty. I hailed him to find an alternative route. As he approached he was saying:

"Sorry. You can't go through, the bomb is likely to go off at any minute now."

On reaching my car he looked inside and noticing my uniform, stood back and said:

"I'm very sorry, sir. I didn't know you were a wing commander. It is quite all right for you to go through."

Professor John Frank Adams, F.R.S., M.A., Ph.D.,
Professor of Astronomy and Geometry, University of Cambridge.

There was a university in New England where the students operated a "bank" of term papers and other homework assignments. There were papers to suit all needs; it would look odd if an undistinguished student suddenly handed in a brilliant essay, so there were papers for an A grade, papers for a B and papers for a C. The papers guaranteed to get a safe and inconspicuous C were as popular as any.

In this university there was also a student who had spent the weekend on pursuits other than homework; so he went to the bank. His course was a standard one, and the bank had several papers which had stood the test of time. He drew out a paper for a C, retyped it, and handed his work in.

In due course he received it back with comments in red ink and they went as follows:

"I wrote this paper myself twenty years ago. I always thought it should have had an A, and now I am glad to give it one."

Sir Godfrey Agnew, K.C.V.O., C.B.,
Clerk of the Privy Council, 1953-74.

A man decides to spend a lazy week-end reading, goes to a bookshop and selects a book entitled "How to Hug". His disappointment can be imagined when he realised, when unwrapping it at home, that it was Volume VI of the Encyclopaedia Britannica.

A woman commissioned an artist to paint her portrait for a fee of £300. She immediately wrote out a cheque and handed it to him.

Artist: "I thought we had agreed a fee of £300 but you have made out your cheque for £400."

Woman: "Yes, I know; but I find it a bit embarrassing. Would you have any objection to painting me in the nude?"

Artist: "None whatsoever provided I can keep my socks on as I must have somewhere to put my brushes."

A lost and exhausted climber was walking across a snow plateau when he suddenly became aware of a strong smell of fish and chips. Through the mist ahead he sees a Monastery and a priest standing in the doorway.

"You must be the Friar."

"No he's the frier and I am the chip monk."

Control to pilot: "What is your height and position?"
Pilot: "I'm 5ft 8in and I'm sitting down."

Lord Airedale,
A Deputy Speaker, House of Lords.

When Harold Larwood was in his heyday he magnanimously gave up his rest-day in the middle of an important match to take part in a Sunday charity game. The umpire had some unexplained grudge against Larwood. Early in the innings Larwood sent down a dead-straight medium-paced ball, which the batsman intercepted with his pad.

"How's that?" said Larwood.

"Not out," said the umpire.

With a shrug of his shoulders Larwood bowled a noticeably faster ball, just wide of the off-stump. The batsman snicked it, and the wicket-keeper caught it.

"How's that?" said Larwood.

"Not out," said the umpire.

Wearing an expression which denoted that this practice would now cease, Larwood took his full run and sent down his fastest ball. Straight as an arrow it sped. The stumps were spread-eagled; the bails shot over the wicket-keeper's head and came to rest half-way to the boundary.

Said Larwood to the umpire:

"I darned-near bowled him that time."

Sir Lawrence Airey, K.C.B.,
Chairman, Board of Inland Revenue.

There was this chap who had a great deal of trouble getting in touch with his firm of solicitors — a city firm with three partners, Smith, Brown & Robinson. Whenever he rang to speak to one of the partners they were unavailable. He would be told that "Mr. Smith was in the courts, Mr. Brown was on an overseas visit, and Mr. Robinson was tied up". Next time it was Mr. Smith who was abroad, Mr. Brown was in the courts, and Mr. Robinson was tied up!

This went on until eventually he expostulated:

"Look, I can understand that if a partner is out of the office, or abroad, I can't speak to him, but what about the partner who is in — how is it that Mr. Robinson always seems to be tied up?"

"Oh, you don't understand, sir. You see, whenever Mr. Smith and Mr.

Brown have to be out of the office together, they always tie up Mr. Robinson!"

Sir Geoffrey Aldington, K.B.E., C.M.G.,
H.M. Ambassador to Luxembourg, 1961-66.

A woman who worked among children in the Middle East drove herself about her district by jeep, and was one day annoyed to find that not only had she run out of petrol, but that the spare jerrican she usually carried, was missing from the vehicle. However, she remembered that she had passed a petrol station a mile or so back, and being a woman of resource, she took out the only receptacle she had suitable for her purpose, a child's chamber-pot, trudged back to the garage, had the vessel filled, and trudged back to her stranded jeep.

When she had unscrewed the petrol tank cap and, with some difficulty, was pouring the contents of her pot into the tank, she became aware that an enormous Cadillac, full of wealthy oil-sheiks, had stopped on the road beside her jeep, and the occupants were observing her with much interest. Eventually one of the Arabs got out and came over to her.

"Excuse me, Sister," he said courteously, "My friends and I would like to assure you that, although we obviously do not share your religion, we greatly admire your faith."

Lord Alexander of Potterhill, L.H.D., Ph.D., M.Ed., M.A., B.Sc.,
General Secretary, Association of Education Committees, 1945-77.

Standing in the queue to attend a football match in Belfast, I overheard the following conversation:

"How are you Paddy?" says Mick, "And how is that nice little boy of yours?"

"Oh," says Paddy, "he's fine, but unfortunately he took the 11+ examination a few weeks ago and he's failed."

"What a terrible thing that is," says Mick.

"Oh," says Paddy, "it's worse than that, Mick — if he'd just been born a day later he could have had another go at it next year."

''Isn't that the damnedest thing,'' says Mick, ''and it's just that kind of thing you don't think about at the time.''

Captain John Steele Allan, C.B.E., Company Director.

At camp the orderly officer of my regiment was on his rounds one day to find out whether there were any complaints. The men were having their mid-day meal and the officer said:

''Any complaints?''

''Yes, sir,'' said Private Thomson.

''Well!'' said the officer, ''what is your complaint?''

''Too much sand in the soup, sir,'' replied Private Thomson.

The officer said sternly:

''You have joined this regiment to serve your Country, understand.''

''Yes, sir, to serve my Country but not to eat it.''

Sir Donald Allen, O.B.E., M.C., Clerk to the Trustees of London Parochial Charities, 1930-65.

In church one Sunday morning a mother was kneeling with her small son during prayers and the boy was laughing very loudly. The mother said:

''Johnny stop making that noise.''

The little boy replied:

''It is all right, mummy, I have just told God a joke and we are both laughing.''

Lord Allen (now Lord Croham), G.C.B., F.B.I.M., F.R.S.A., Head of Home Civil Service, 1974-77.

A vicar called on an old lady who was one of his parishioners and was very impressed by her talking parrot. But he noticed that the bird had a blue ribbon tied to each leg and asked the lady why.

"If I pull the ribbon on his right leg," she said, "he sings me a jolly hymn tune — Onward Christian Soldiers — but if I am in a sad mood, I pull the ribbon on his left leg and he suits my mood by singing — Abide With Me."

"Truly remarkable," said the vicar. "And what if you pull both ribbons at once?"

"Then I fall off my perch, you silly old fool," said the parrot.

Professor George Allen, C.B.E., F.B.A., Emeritus Professor of Political Economy, University of London.

There was once a Chinese sage whose chief doctrine was that the supernatural was impossible. He had a son who was a faithful disciple. The sage died and the son kept vigil by his father's coffin. Suddenly, in the middle of the night, the coffin rose in the air and remained suspended between floor and ceiling. The son was immeasurably distressed. Filial piety enjoined him to believe that the supernatural was impossible but the evidence of his senses contradicted this proposition.

In his perplexity he prayed to the spirit of his father, saying:

"Father, do not, I beg you, destroy my belief in the impossibility of the supernatural."

At once the coffin descended slowly to the floor and the son's faith in the father's doctrine was restored.

Lord Allen of Abbeydale, G.C.B., Member, Security Commission.

A Yorkshire terrier and a Russian borzoi were waiting side by side outside Harrods for their mistresses, and naturally fell into conversation.

"Have you always lived in London?" asked the terrier.

"Oh no," said the borzoi, "I was brought up in Russia and in fact have spent most of my life there!"

"And what was life like over there?" asked the terrier.

"It was pretty good," said the borzoi, "I had a thermostatically heated kennel, mink-lined blankets and bones dipped in caviare (of which I am particularly fond)."

"Dear me," said the terrier, "Then why on earth did you come and live over here?"

"It's perfectly true that I don't have these comforts here," said the borzoi, "but the fact is, I do like to bark occasionally."

Rear-Admiral Courtney Anderson, C.B.,
Flag Officer, Admiralty Interview Board, 1969-71.

Those of you who speak Spanish, will, of course, know the old Castilian proverb that an after-dinner speech is like the horns of a bull — with a point here . . . . and a point there . . . . and an awful lot of bull in between . . . .

An old woman was sitting alone with her cat polishing her lamp, when there was a sudden puff of smoke and a genii appeared and offered her three wishes. The old woman thought quickly and then said:

"I'd like to be rich, I'd like to be young again, and I'd like my cat to turn into a handsome prince."

Another puff of smoke and she found herself young and glamorous in a beautiful evening gown. The cat had disappeared but a gorgeous prince stood beside her, holding out his arms. As she melted into his embrace he murmured softly into her ear:

"Now I bet you're sorry you took me to the vet for that little operation."

I will, at least try and be brief — brevity exemplified in a certain Court when the convicted prisoner cried:

"As God is my Judge, my Lord, I am not guilty."

To which the Judge replied tersely:

"He's not, I am, you are, six months."

The Late Sir Eric Ansorge, C.S.I., C.I.E., Indian Civil Service, 1910-46.

The dean was very thrilled by the fact that his wife had written a book; that she had also presented him with a son ranked only second in his estimation, so that when a friend came up and shook him by the hand to congratulate him on his son and heir saying:

"Congratulations, Mr. Dean."

The dean replied:

"Yes, I consider it a very estimable performance on the part of my wife considering that I gave her no assistance and she had very little help except from the minor canon."

Sir John Arbuthnot, Bt., M.B.E., T.D., A Church Commissioner for England, 1962-77.

An English lady travelling in Germany left a valuable fur coat in charge of a German woman in the carriage. When she returned, the German was wearing the coat, and said that it belonged to her. The guard tried in vain to discover to which of the two it belonged, and finally sent them off to the Consul. The Consul asked to examine the coat, and brought it back a few moments later saying:

"This is a very serious affair; whoever the coat belongs to has been smuggling cocaine. Here are the two packets I found in the coat."

The German woman excused herself and bowed herself out of the room, saying:

"Just my little joke."

The English woman said:

"I can't understand how they could have got there."

The Consul replied:

"Don't worry, it is only salt, that I put there to find out whose coat it really was."

Orders of advancement in the Civil Service:—

C.M.G. Call me God

K.C.M.G. Keep calling me God

G.C.M.G. God calls me God.

The Viscount of Arbuthnott, D.S.C.,
Lord Lieutenant Grampian Region; Landowner and Farmer.

A mighty Red Indian chief had married three wives and allocated a wigwam to each of them. He promised that he would provide them with any sort of bed covering they wanted. The first and oldest, who was a well brought up and practical girl, asked for the hide of a buffalo, which was easily obtained. The second, who was intelligent but daring, wished for the pelt of a bear. This was a little harder and more dangerous for him but was nevertheless soon brought to her. The third wife was much the prettiest and most vivacious and she asked for the skin of a hippopotamus, which was a real challenge, but he finally succeeded in getting her one.

Nine months later the first wife had a boy, the second had a girl and the third had twins, a boy *and* a girl, which only goes to confirm that the squaw on the hippopotamus is always equal to the squaw on the other two hides.

A little girl was asked to prepare a short story which introduced the word frugal. She went home and found that the dictionary meaning gave conserve or save as the essence of being frugal.

"Once upon a time there was a beautiful princess who was riding her horse beside the river when it slipped and she fell into the rushing water. Just then a handsome prince rode by and she called out, 'Frugal me, frugal me' so he got off his horse and he frugalled her and they lived happily ever after!"

The Rt. Hon. Peter Archer, Q.C., M.P.,
Solicitor-General, 1974-79.

At the annual dinner of the Central Borneo branch of a well-known organisation, they were celebrating the end of the president's year of office.

Half way through the second course, one member turned to his neighbour and said:

"I know I shouldn't say this, but I don't like our old president."

The neighbour replied cheerfully:

"Then just eat the vegetables."

A friend of mine who is responsible for replacing domestic gas appliances in preparation for natural gas, was visited by an unhappy looking old lady.

"They have just installed a new cooker for me," she said. "Please can I have my old cooker back?"

"But," he said, "I have seen the new type of cooker. It has every possible convenience. Many people would give anything for a cooker like that."

"I know," she said. "It's lovely, but please can I have my old one back."

"Of course, I understand that the new one seems strange to you, but it is very simple to operate. I am sure you will be able to manage it very quickly," he said.

"Oh," she said, "I know I could learn to use it in no time, but please can I have my old one back?"

"But," he said, "if you think the new cooker is lovely, and you are sure you will learn to use it, why are you so anxious to have your old one back?"

"My dinner is inside it."

John Arlott, O.B.E.,
Broadcaster and Author on Cricket and Wine.

In a local cricket match a batsman was given "out" in an atrocious l.b.w. decision. As he passed the umpire who had given him out, he said:

"I wasn't out, you know."

The umpire could not resist the old, hackneyed retort:

"Oh weren't you, well, you look in 'The Chronicle' next Friday and see whether you were or not."

Before he could enjoy his triumph the batsman answered:
"No, *you* look — I am the editor of 'The Chronicle'."

Professor Sir Alfred Ayer, F.B.A.,
Professor of Logic in the University of Oxford, 1959-78.

It is related of Oscar Wilde that he was standing aloof at a party when his hostess came up to him and asked him anxiously:
"Are you enjoying yourself, Mr. Wilde?"
"Yes, I am," he said. "There is nothing else here to enjoy."

(Similar stories, but ascribed to George Bernard Shaw, have been sent by other contributors.)

Lord Aylestone, C.H., P.C., C.B.E.,
Chairman, Independent Broadcasting Authority, 1967-75.

A Member of Parliament after a series of all night sittings ran into trouble with his wife who doubted whether he spent all those hours in the House of Commons. On arriving home very early one morning he found a note left for him which read:
"The day before yesterday you came home yesterday morning, yesterday you came home this morning, so if today you come home tomorrow morning, you will find that I left you yesterday."

Within a few hours of the death of a Member of Parliament, a very eager prospective candidate telephoned the National Agent as follows:
"I was very sorry to hear of the death of Tom Atkins, is there any chance of me taking his place?"
The National Agent replied:
"Yes, if the undertaker has no objection."

Three elderly men discussing death and the after life were telling each other how they would like to leave this life, as follows:—

1st old man: "I would like to die climbing Everest after planting a flag on the summit."

2nd old man: "I would like to die bowling the last ball down in a vital test match."

3rd old man: "I would like to die in bed, shot by a jealous husband."

Sir Vahé Bairamian,
Editor of Publications on Law; Justice, Supreme Court of Nigeria, 1960-68.

When a diplomat says yes, he means perhaps; when he says perhaps, he means no; and if he says no, he is not a diplomat.

When a lady says no, she means perhaps; when she says perhaps, she means yes; and if she says yes, she is not a lady.

The police caught Sam gambling in his flat; the others escaped; him they took to Court and charged with playing a game of chance, but he would not admit it.

"But, Sam," said the sergeant, "here are the cards and the money we picked up from the table; why don't you admit it?"

"I can't," said Sam.

"Why can't you?" asked the angry beak.

"Your Honour, I can't," said Sam. "I wasn't playing a game of chance; I had marked all the cards."

The Rt. Hon. Sir George Baker, O.B.E.,
President of the Family Division of the High Court of Justice, 1971-79.

When I first became a judge and had to try divorce cases, I thought incompatibility was the main rock on which marriages foundered, until one of my older and wiser brethren put me right.

"Incompatibility," he explained to me, "is the corner stone, the cement of marriage — so long as the husband has the income, and the wife the patability."

The Late Air Chief Marshal Sir John Baker, G.B.E., K.C.B., M.C., D.F.C., Controller of Aircraft, Ministry of Supply, 1953-56.

Sing hey diddle diddle
a middle-aged fiddle
can still play a jolly good tune,
and always remember
a rose in December
is a great deal more fun than in June.

The Late Sir Michael Balcon, Film Producer.

Whenever Louis B. Mayer went off on a trip to Europe, he loved to make a big fuss about it, with a party — and a presentation.

The presentation took place on a very hot day in a crowded bungalow on the studio lot. We were served with warm inferior champagne and the proceedings began. On the day of the presentation Louis B. Mayer had had a very big lunch of noodles (known to be his favourite food) and then hurried to the ceremony.

The atmosphere in the bungalow was suffocating. The moment came for Louis B. Mayer to make his speech of thanks but he had not got far with it when suddenly he collapsed in a dead faint.

We all rushed around and achieved nothing until his friend Frank Orsalte (head of a talent agency) had the reasonable idea of fetching the studio doctor. He ran out of the room but what he forgot in the excitement was that his exit was the signal he had arranged with the studio orchestra, which was waiting outside to do their bit. They started up vigorously with "For He's a Jolly Good Fellow" whilst Mayer lay out for the count on the bungalow floor.

As there was nothing more wrong with Mayer than the effects of gluttony and heat it was a typically ridiculous, if somewhat macabre scene.

Lord Balfour of Inchyre, P.C., M.C., Parliamentary Under-Secretary of State for Air, 1938-44; Minister Resident in West Africa, 1944-45.

There was a certain civil servant who had spent all his life preparing replies to Parliamentary questions. On holiday on Dartmoor he was caught by a night fog. A motor car stopped and its driver called out:

"Where am I?"

The civil servant replied, "In a car", and started to walk on.

The motorist complained of the paucity of the reply.

"My reply was accurate. It has all the elements of a correct reply. It is brief. It is true; and adds nothing to the information already available. Goodnight."

Sir John Balfour, G.C.M.G., G.B.E.,
British Ambassador to Argentina, 1948-51, and Spain, 1951-54.

During the last war the milkmaid at our family home-farm in Berwickshire announced one day to my sister-in-law that she was thinking of leaving her job because her boss Jimmie, the byre-man, or herdsman, had given her no word of encouragement during the six months in which she had worked for him. My sister-in-law therefore interviewed Jimmie and asked him whether he was satisfied with the girl's work.

"Aye," he replied, "I'm weel satisfied."

"Then do say something to her," pleaded my sister-in-law, "she is so discouraged by your silence that she is thinking of going away."

"I'll dae ma best," quoth Jimmie, "but sometimes as much as three weeks gaes by and I dinna even speak tae a coo."

Question: "How do you recognise a Scottish ship?"
Answer: "Because it is not followed by seagulls."

The Late Air Vice-Marshal Sir Ben Ball, K.B.E., C.B.,
Air Officer Commanding-in-Chief, Royal Air Force Signals Command, 1966-68.

How to distinguish lady lawyers?
Those with briefs are barristers. Those without briefs are solicitors!

Sir Joseph Balmer, J.P.,
Lord Mayor of Birmingham, 1954-55.

Advert in South African paper:
"Lady who has cast off clothing of all descriptions invites inspection."

Lord Barber, P.C., T.D.,
Chancellor of the Exchequer, 1970-74.

At a time when Winston Churchill was in the political wilderness, Bernard Shaw sent him four tickets for the first night of his new play, explaining in the covering letter that they were "for you and your friends — if you have any".

Churchill replied that he was returning the tickets because unfortunately he was already engaged on that evening, but would very much like to have tickets "for the second night — if there is one".

The Rt. Rev. C.K.N. Bardsley, C.B.E., D.D.,
Bishop of Coventry, 1956-76.

Two old sweats were sitting in a shell hole on Anzio Beach. The shells were coming over thick and fast. One turned to the other and he said:

"Lofty, I'm scared stiff. Let's have a prayer."

"Prayer?" said the other, "What do you think this is, a Sunday school outing?"

Time passed by and the shells came still more thick and fast, bombs began to fall and it became hell let loose; whereupon the one turned to the other and he said:

"Lofty, I think we're in for a packet. Do you know any hymns?"

"Hymns?" said the other, "What do you think I am, an opera star?"

Ten more minutes went by and they thought that their last moment had come; whereupon the fellow took off his tin helmet, turned eyes to heaven and said:

"Lofty, I suggest that we do something religious — let's have a collection."

The Late Sir Robert Barlow,
Industrialist.

Scene: Supermarket in U.S.A.

Salesman: Offering greens peas in the pod.

Customer: "Gee! I've had them dried, frozen, packaged in cartons, and canned. Whatever will they think up next?"

Sir Henry Barnard,
Judge of the High Court of Justice, 1944-59; Admiralty Judge of the Cinque Ports.

A man was feeling very peculiar — so peculiar, that he sent for the doctor. The doctor came and gave him a thorough examination. At the end of it he said:

"I have some bad news for you and some good news. The bad news is that you are in for a change of sex."

"My God," said the man.

The doctor quickly intervened and said:

"Now for the good news; this will entitle you to play off the ladies' tees."

Sir Cecil Bateman, K.B.E.,
Retired Civil Servant; Director of Allied Irish Banks, 1970-80.

The old clergyman was without doubt the world's worst golfer. One day, on a fairly long straight hole he uncorked a towering drive straight towards the pin. The ball started to roll and as if drawn by a magnet continued to roll — over the apron — across the green — hit the pin and dropped into the hole.

The astounded clergyman turned his eyes towards heaven.

"Lord," he begged, "I'd rather do it *myself*."

Major-General Stuart Battye, C.B., M.A., F.R.S.A.,
Director of Movements, War Office, 1958-61; Director, Council for Small Industries in Rural Areas, 1963-73.

Derek Wisbey, a senior thatching officer, relates the following:

Thatchers have a great reputation for being men of action and very few words. In Devon a well-known character was industriously thatching a house, right up on the ridge, when a newly appointed vicar passed and tried to get to know a possible new parishioner. A series of "Conversation openers" were addressed to the thatcher in particular and presumably the sky in general... "Nice day for the time of year" . . . "Is it very draughty up there?" . . . "How is the straw crop this year?" . . . and so on . . . all without response. Thatchers doubtless have to keep their minds on their job and not turn round to chat on tall pole ladders.

Eventually the silent one returned to earth and the vicar, nothing daunted, pointed to his own shining bald pate, surrounded by a scant fringe of white hair, and said:

"Can you do anything about this with your thatch?"

Still mute the thatcher came up to the vicar and, to his astonishment, solemnly went round him, turning up the fringe of white hair and peering under it with professional appraisal. At last he spoke.

"Can't do nothing for you, vicar," he said, "timbers are all rotten."

**Lord Beaumont of Whitley, M.A.,
President of the Liberal Party, 1969-70.**

The late Noël Coward was taking one of his young godchildren for a walk when they saw two dogs mating.

"Oh, Uncle Noël, look at those dogs! What are they doing?"

"Well, one poor little doggie has gone blind and the other is pushing him all the way to St. Dunstan's."

**Sir Terence Beckett, C.B.E.,
Director, C.B.I.**

Planning a new motor car is like making love to an elephant.

If you are successful nothing happens for two years, and if you are not you get trampled to death.

**Leslie Herbert Bedford, C.B.E.,
Formerly Director of Engineering, Guided Weapons Division, British Aircraft Corporation.**

The visiting school inspector decided to take over a class which happened to be engaged on a Bible Study period. Selecting an encouraging looking boy in the front row, he said:

"Your name?'

"Smith, sir."

"Right, Smith. Now tell me, who blew down the walls of Jericho?"

"Please, sir, I didn't."

The inspector was angry at this cheeky answer and reported to the head.

The head said:

"Ah, Smith! Well I happen to know Smith very well. He is a good and truthful boy, and you can take it from me that if he says he didn't do it then he certainly didn't do it."

The inspector was even more incensed and duly reported the entire incident to the District Chief Education Officer.

The latter considered the situation and said:

"Well, in a case like this, I think we should take a broad view. Tell them to get an estimate for the repairs and I'll authorise it."

Sir Gawain Bell, K.C.M.G., C.B.E.,
Secretary-General South Pacific Commission, 1966-70.

A Catholic priest was driving a devout but somewhat simple member of his congregation along a lonely road in the Republic of Ireland when he ran over a hare. The priest stopped the car and walked back along the road to where the hare lay inert and apparently dead. He then returned to the car, opened his suitcase, extracted a bottle of liquid and, with his companion, retraced his steps to where the hare lay. He uncorked the bottle and sprinkled a few drops of the liquid over the hare.

The hare's ears moved and it showed signs of life. A few more drops were sprinkled over the animal which then sat up and looked around. A third and final application of the liquid resulted in the hare's loping off over the fields and away.

"Sure, Your Reverence," whispered his companion with undisguised awe, "that must have been very Holy Water."

"Not at all, not at all," replied the priest. "Why, 'twas simply Hare Restorer."

The Hon. Sir George Bellew, K.C.B., K.C.V.O., F.S.A.,
Garter Principal King of Arms, 1950-61; Secretary of the Order of the Garter, 1961-74.

Strawberries also have their little problems.

For example, one strawberry said to another on a certain sad occasion:

"If we hadn't been in the same bed we wouldn't both be in this jam now."

Sir Robert Bellinger, G.B.E.,
Lord Mayor of London, 1966-67; Governor, B.B.C., 1968-71.

A wealthy man was advised by his bank manager that he had an overdraft of £100 and that interest would be charged at 12% per annum. The client insisted that he should deposit his Rolls-Royce car as security and drove it to the bank leaving it in the adjacent car park. A month later he returned to collect the car.

The curious bank manager asked him why he had insisted on depositing the car for security. The client with the overdraft replied:

"Where can you get car parking for a month for £1?"

Nicholas Bethell,
Author and Translator; Member of European Parliament.

Waiter: "How would you like your coffee, sir?"

Diner (who has dined well): "Waiter, let me tell you something. I like my coffee the same way as I like my women — hot, strong and sweet."

Waiter (deadpan): "Black or white, sir?"

Eric Raymond Bevington, C.M.G.,
H.M. Colonial Administrative Service, 1935-62.

An elderly representative of the race of the Children of Israel, full of years was lying in bed dying. He had obeyed all the commands of Jehovah and had been fruitful and had multiplied.

As his life ebbed away, his failing eyes told him that the family were gathered round the bed but they were only hazy and indistinguishable forms. So he asked:

"Abraham, my boy, are you there?" "Yes, Father, I am here."
"Reuben boy, are you there?" "Yes, Father, I am here."
"Jacob, are you there?" "Yes, Father, I am here."
"Rachel are you there?" "Yes, Father, I am here."
"Ephraim are you there?" "Yes, Father, I am here."
"Leah, dear, are you there?" "Yes, Father, I am here."
"Esau are you there?" "Yes, Father, I am here."
"Moses, my son, are you there?" "Yes, Father, I am here."
"Joseph, are you there?" "Yes, Father, I am here."
"Sarah, my dear wife, are you there?" "Yes, Yes, I am here."

The old man counted on his fingers, thought a moment, made an effort to sit up, and in great anxiety called out:

"Benjamin, are you here too?" "Yes, Father, I am here."

"Then who is looking after the business?" cried the old man with his last breath.

John Benjamin Bibby, J.P.,
Chairman, J. Bibby & Sons Ltd.

A shopkeeper noticed that a Scots customer was counting his change very carefully and seemed rather dubious about it.

"What's the matter, sir," he said, "your change is right, isn't it?"

"Aye," replied the Scotsman, "but it's only just right."

A golfer had a very dour Scots caddie. He was playing very badly and, to hide his embarrassment, as he was about to take his fifth shot out of a bunker he said to the caddie:

"Well caddie, golf's a funny game, isn't it?"

"Aye," said the caddie, "but it's no meant to be."

Lord Birdwood,
Executive Search Consultant.

If at first you don't succeed your successor will.

**Professor John Howard Birkinshaw, D.Sc., F.R.I.C.,
Emeritus Professor of Biochemistry, University of London.**

A physicist had a horseshoe hanging on the door of his laboratory. His colleagues were surprised and asked whether he believed that it would bring luck to his experiments.

He answered:

"No, I don't believe in superstitions. But I have been told that it works even if you don't believe in it!"

**The Hon. Lord Birsay, K.T., C.B.E., T.D., Q.C.,
Chairman, Scottish Land Court.**

"Maun, Angus, did you hear Donald's deed?"

"No, maun, d'ye tell me!"

"Aye, he's deed. An' he left Thirty Thoosan' Poonds."

"No, maun. Kennin' Donald, he didna *leave* it. He was taken awa' frae it!"

**Sir Cyril Black, D.L., J.P.,
Member of Parliament for Wimbledon, 1950-70.**

The most popular after-dinner speech on record was made by a man dining with his wife alone in the privacy of their home, and it consisted of one sentence containing seven words of one syllable:

"You leave them, dear, I'll do them."

**The Rt. Hon. David Bleakley, M.A.,
Northern Ireland Politician; Educationalist and Broadcaster.**

The Perils of Logic:

The professor, wishing to establish a link between cause and effect, produced a flea to demonstrate his point. Placing the flea on the lectern he called on it to jump. And the flea jumped. Whereupon the great man produced a scalpel and cut off the flea's legs. The command "jump" was then repeated. And this time the flea remained stationary.

In triumph, the professor proclaimed to his students:

"My dear friends, we have now proved conclusively that when the legs of a flea are amputated the creature is rendered completely deaf!"

Dr. Walter Fred Bodmer, F.R.S.,
Director of Research, Imperial Cancer Research Fund.

Genetics is an area that in many people's minds raises rather frightening social problems for our society, fears which are fed by such journalistic phrases as "genetic engineering" and "test-tube babies". This was brought home to me rather vividly when I was returning with my family from a holiday on the Continent the summer before last. As we were confidently driving out along the "Nothing to declare" customs lane we were stopped by a rather severe-looking customs officer. Having seen from my passport that I was a professor, he asked me first what university I was at.

"Oxford," I said, confidently hoping that that at least would placate him.

However, next came the question:

"What's your subject?"

"Genetics," I said.

Silence followed for a brief moment, then:

"Hm, I'd better let you go hadn't I, otherwise you might turn me into a frog."

Sir Adrian Boult, C.H., M.A., D.Mus., F.R.C.M.,
Composer and Conductor; Vice-President,
Council of the Royal College of Music.

One day I was rehearsing an orchestra, and I noticed one of the players had a nasty cough. A glass of water was handed along to him, and I thought no more of it until I noticed quite a disturbance round him, and a good many smiles. I knew, but didn't remember at the moment, that the gentleman concerned had a good thirst of his own, and I shouted out:

"What is the matter? Haven't you people ever seen a man drink a glass of water before?"

I chose my words badly: the answering chorus came back to me with superb ensemble:

"NOT THAT MAN!"

General Lord Bourne, G.C.B., K.B.E., C.M.G.,
General Officer Commanding British Sector, Berlin, 1949-51; Director of Military Operations, Malaya, 1954-56; Commandant Imperial Defence College, 1958-59.

My wife and I had a No. 1 boy in Hong Kong years ago. We didn't know he was married and he never took leave. So I was a little surprised when Ah Hing said he wanted leave to go to Canton where his wife had just had a baby son.

He came back on the Monday. The following Friday he again asked for leave to go to Canton. I said:

"But, Ah Hing, you went to Canton last week — is your wife all right, is the baby all right?"

"Yes," said Ah Hing, "They all velly well. I likee go makee another one."

Viscount Boyd of Merton, C.H., P.C., D.L.,
Secretary of State for the Colonies, 1954-59.

Some time during the Lloyd George War Government, when Maurice Hankey was Secretary to the Cabinet, the Prime Minister, after a long discussion, took his colleagues to dinner. When he left he said to Maurice Hankey:

"You know, Maurice, what we have agreed. Do a note."

When they got back Hankey's note read as follows:

"Now while the great ones depart for their dinner
The Secretary stays on growing thinner and thinner;
Racking his brains to record and report
What he thinks they think that they ought to have thought!"

The Late Brigadier Sir John Boyd, O.B.E., F.R.S., M.D., F.R.C.P., D.P.H.,
Member, Colonial Medical Research Committee, 1945-60; Chairman, Research Defence Society, 1956-68.

Andrew was a little boy aged 8, the son of strict Presbyterian parents who doted on him. He was a very good little boy who did well both at day school and Sunday school, where he sang like a cherub. But one morning he apparently got out of bed on the wrong side, and came down to breakfast in a very cantankerous mood. At his place on the table was a plate of prunes.

"I don't want prunes," he said.

"Andrew," said his mother, "you must eat your prunes."

"I don't want prunes," said Andrew.

"Andrew," said his mother in stern tones, "eat your prunes."

"I won't," said Andrew angrily.

"Andrew," said his mother, "you must not speak to your mother in that way. God has commanded little boys to honour their parents, and will punish those who do not." But Andrew was unmoved, and the prunes went back to the pantry uneaten.

Late that evening, after Andrew had gone to bed and while his parents were sitting by the fire downstairs, a thunderstorm blew up from the horizon. Gradually the lightning became more vivid and the thunder louder. In an interval between flashes, the parents heard Andrew's bedroom door open and footsteps come down the stairs and go into the pantry.

"Ah," said the delighted mother, "how wonderful. Now he has had his lesson."

At that moment there was an even more brilliant flash, and a deafening peal which shook the house. As the reverberations died away, Andrew's sweet little voice was heard coming from the pantry.

"Hell of a fuss about a few bloody prunes."

Lord Boyd-Carpenter, P.C., D.L.,
Chairman, Rugby Portland Cement.

Man leaving his home for a stag dinner, is challenged by his wife with the question.

"What would you do if you found me in bed with another man when you come back?"

He replied, without hesitation:

"Do? I would break his white stick, and shoot his guide-dog."

Marshal of the Royal Air Force Sir Dermot Boyle, G.C.B., K.C.V.O., K.B.E., A.F.C.,
Chief of Air Staff, 1956-59; Vice-Chairman, British Aircraft Corporation, 1962-71.

During the war a man being medically examined for military service had to be rejected because all the tests the eye-specialist applied seemed to indicate that the man was virtually blind.

The specialist felt that in some way he had been tricked and he was convinced of this when he called in at the Victoria Station News Cinema and found himself sitting next to the cause of his doubts. The specialist was looking around to find a military policeman to arrest the culprit, when the man put his hand on the specialist's arm and said:

"Excuse me, madam, can you tell me if this bus goes to Victoria?"

An Irish boss trying to resist engaging a would-be employee.

"The trouble is, Paddy, I haven't enough work to keep you busy."

Reply: "Ah, sir, it is very little would keep me busy."

Lord Brabourne,
Film and Television Producer.

A great friend of mine, who lived in the country, was invited to a wedding in London. One of her relations died and the funeral was fixed on the same day as the wedding and only an hour or two before the service. This placed her in rather a predicament as obviously the bright clothes which were suitable for a wedding would be unsuitable for a funeral and there was no time to change in between.

However, she decided to solve the problem by wearing a smart black suit for both occasions with a black hat for the funeral and to take a very gay flowered hat for the wedding. This she carried in a brown paper bag and as she arrived only just before the funeral procession at the church, she hurriedly left it in the porch, so that she could pick it up again on her way out. She then went into the church and took her place in one of the pews.

A few minutes later when the coffin was carried up the aisle past her seat she was thunderstruck to see her best wedding hat placed on top of the coffin amongst the other floral tributes from the family. Later still, when the coffin was lowered into the grave, she had to stand by and see her treasured hat disappear forever into the bowels of the earth.

The Late Earl of Bradford, T.D., J.P.,
Crown Estate Commissioner, 1956-67; Vice-Lieutenant of Shropshire, 1970-74.

A Roman Catholic couple living in Birmingham got married. The first year there was a baby. The second year there was a baby. The third year there was no baby.

The young wife went to the confessional and was told by the priest:

"My daughter, you know the rules, don't you?"

"Yes, Father," she said, "I know the rules, but I also know the statistics, and the statisticians say that every third baby born in Birmingham is a black one!"

Colonel Hugh Trefusis Brassey, O.B.E., M.C.,
Vice-Lieutenant of Wiltshire, since 1968; Colonel, The Royal Scots Dragoon Guards, 1974-79.

At one time in the desert war, a German paymaster was captured by soldiers who relieved him of most — if not all — of the pay for the Afrika Corps. Being a very high officer he was sent back to the Corps Commander's Headquarters (I believe it was General Sir Brian Horrocks) where he insisted on seeing the General. This was granted.

After salutations, the paymaster said he particularly wished to say how much he respected the integrity of the British soldier because although he had been relieved of the money, he had been given a receipt. Much surprised the Corps Commander asked if he could see the receipt. It was produced.

It said:

"This old B. had 50,000 marks. Now he hasn't."

The Marquess of Bristol,
Landowner and Industrialist; Hereditary High Steward of the Liberty of St. Edmund.

Man in a pub: "Funny how my wife can spot blonde hairs, and miss garage doors."

The middle-aged woman said proudly to her husband:
"You know dear, I can still get into the same skirts I had before we were married."
The husband replied tersely:
"I wish I could."

The Late Sir Israel Brodie, K.B.E.,
Formerly Chief Rabbi of the United Hebrew Congregations of the British Commonwealth of Nations.

A refugee from the Nazis managed to get to Lisbon. He sought out the American Consul to try and obtain a visa to the United States of America. The Consul asked him where he had come from originally and he said Rumania. When asked whether he was a citizen of Rumania and having replied in the affirmative, the Consul said:
"I am sorry but the quota for immigrants from Rumania is already full up. You will have to wait for another eight years before your request could be considered."
As the refugee reached the door, he turned and asked the Consul whether he would have to come in the morning or in the afternoon.

Sir Paul Bryan, D.S.O., M.C., M.P.,
Minister of State, Department of Employment, 1970-72.

Conjurer to yokel: "Now sir, would you be surprised if I took a rabbit out of your pocket?"
Yokel: "I would that."
Conjurer: "Why would you be surprised?"
Yokel: "'Cos I've got a ruddy ferret in it."

The Duke of Buccleuch and Queensberry, V.R.D.

While I was a Member of Parliament an overseas visitor to the House of Commons was greatly alarmed by the clanging of the Division Bells, indicating a vote, but was calmed by his companion who replied:

"Oh I guess one of them must have escaped."

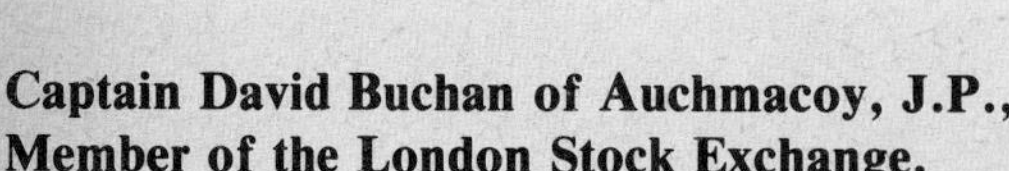

Captain David Buchan of Auchmacoy, J.P., Member of the London Stock Exchange.

The Moderator of the General Assembly of the Church of Scotland was playing a round of golf with the Episcopal Bishop of Aberdeen and nearing the 18th hole their argument as to which was the more like God got steadily more heated. In the end they decided they would ask the first man they met to decide for them. As they approached the club house a figure was seen to stagger down the steps and weave toward them.

"Come here my man," said the Moderator. "His Lordship the Bishop and I wish you to listen to us and then decide which of us is the more like God."

"Oh," said the man, "that's easy, no bother at all, neither of you are because I most clearly am, just follow me and I'll prove it."

Whereupon he swung on his heels, followed by the astonished

prelates, staggered up the steps again, pushed his way through the door, turned straight into the bar and as the barman caught sight of his approach he said:

"Oh, God, not you again!"

A man staggered out of Sothebys with a huge grandfather clock on his shoulder, turned right, heading up Bond Street and knocked a frail old lady clean into the gutter.

She got up, dusted herself down and shouted at the man:

"You stupid idiot, why can't you wear a wrist watch like a civilised human being."

Sir Matt Busby, C.B.E., K.C.S.G.,
Director, Manchester United Football Club.

The after-dinner speaker went on and on until a guest was so fed up he picked up a bottle and aimed it at the speaker's head.

Unfortunately it hit a little man sitting beside him and this knocked him out. Immediately some of the people rushed to bring him round, and when eventually he came round, the only thing he was heard to say was:

"Please hit me again, I can still hear his voice."

Colonel Sir Thomas Pierce Butler, Bt., C.V.O., D.S.O., O.B.E., Resident Governor, Tower of London, 1961-71; Keeper of Jewel House, 1968-71.

One day a friend of mine who had just been appointed head of a big mental establishment near London, asked me if I would like to be taken round. On the appointed day he met me at the big gates and as we walked towards the main building, a man carrying a suitcase was hurrying out. My friend said:

"I would like you to meet Patrick. He has just been discharged after 3 years here."

He called him over and said:

"Patrick, I would like you to meet Colonel Sir Thomas Butler, who is Governor of the Tower of London and Keeper of the Crown Jewels."

Patrick gave me a long, queer look and then said:

"Don't you worry, old man. They will cure you too; when I came here I thought I was the Shah of Persia."

The local vicar had lost his bike and he told his verger that on the following Sunday during his sermon he would bring in the Ten Commandments pausing significantly when he came to "Thou shalt not steal" while the verger studied the faces of the congregation and tried to pick out the culprit. However, during the sermon, the vicar read through the Commandments without a pause.

After the service the verger asked him why he did not pause, to which the vicar replied:

"When I got to 'Thou shalt not commit adultery', I realised where I had left my bike."

Lord Caccia, G.C.M.G., G.C.V.O.,
Provost of Eton, 1965-77.

Sometimes the list of after-dinner speakers is long and it may happen to any of us to be the last on the list. On one such occasion a friend of mine was not able to rise to his feet to propose the health of the society where we were dining until after midnight.

When he did so he held up a sheaf of notes and said:

"I have prepared a speech in which I said a great many flattering things about this society and the splendid work which it does. I am going to give these to your secretary to circulate them or dispose of them as he thinks fit. Meanwhile I should like to thank you for your generous, indeed perhaps over generous, hospitality and at this late hour only add that by now I am too tired and you are too tight. Or is it the other way round?"

At which he sat down to the immense relief of all present.

The Late Sir Sydney Caffyn, C.B.E.,
Member, Industrial Court, 1959-71.

A party of scientists from Russia recently visited this country and the astronomers among them came down to the Royal Observatory at Herstmonceux.

They were shown the giant Isaac Newton telescope and one of them asked that it should be trained on to a particular portion of the sky. Looking through it and examining what he could see, he suddenly exclaimed:

"It is going to rain."

The Royal Observatory staff who were conducting the Russians around were astonished at this remark and wondered if the Russians had really discovered some means of telling the weather by examining a section of the sky through a telescope. They asked him how he could tell it was going to rain and the distinguished astronomer replied:

"My corns hurt."

The Rt. Hon. Sir David Cairns,
A Lord Justice of Appeal, 1970 77.

I was trying a divorce suit and when the wife petitioner was in the witness box I asked her:

"If your present marriage is dissolved would you like to marry again?"

She answered:

"No — but thank you very much."

The Rt. Hon. James Callaghan, M.P.,
Formerly Prime Minister.

Sir William Joynson-Hicks was born plain William Hicks, but he married an heiress by the name of Grace Joynson and hyphenated her name with his own, so becoming William Joynson-Hicks. Joynson-Hicks was a Conservative Member of Parliament who was much opposed to the radical budgets introduced by David Lloyd George nearly 70 years ago when he was Chancellor of the Exchequer.

During the debate, he interrupted Lloyd George whilst he was speaking from the Despatch Box:

"Will the Rt. Hon. Gentleman define what he means by the term unearned increment?"

David Lloyd George looked at him, thought for a moment and replied:

"Yes, I will: unearned increment is the hyphen in the Hon. Gentleman's name."

Montague Calman, F.R.S.A., M.J.I.,
Scriptwriter.

An Englishman, a Frenchman and a Russian were trying to define true happiness.

"True happiness," said the Englishman, "is when you return home tired after work and find a gin and tonic waiting for you."

"You English have no romance," countered the Frenchman, "True happiness is when you go on a business trip, find a pretty girl who entertains you, and then you part without regrets."

"You are both wrong," concluded the Russian. "Real true happiness is when you are home in bed at four o'clock in the morning and there is a hammering at the front door and there stand members of the Secret Police, who say to you, 'Ivan Ivanovitch, you are under arrest', and you are able to reply, 'Sorry! Ivan Ivanovitch lives next door!'."

Wyn Calvin,
Television Artiste.

There is only one *ideal* after-dinner speech — and it consists of just five words:

"I will take the bill!"

Lord Campbell of Eskan,
Chairman, Commonwealth Sugar Exporters' Association; Milton Keynes Development Corporation; Statesman Publishing Company.

Some years ago I was bathing on the Atlantic coast of France and suddenly realised that I was being dragged out to sea by the undertow. I am a very bad swimmer and started yelling desperately for help in bad French:

"Aidez moi — je vais mourir!"

Whereupon four God-like lifesavers swam out and rescued me.

As they were hauling me up the beach, white, feeble and shaking, my seven-year old daughter trotted up to me and said:

"Daddy, why are you helping those men?"

An Englishman, a Frenchman and a German were arguing about the respective merits of their languages.

The Frenchman was saying that French was the language of love, the language of romance, the most beautiful and pure language in the world.

The German was asserting that German was the most vigorous language, the language of philosophers, the language of Goëthe, the language most adaptable to the modern world of science and technology.

When the Englishman's turn came, he said:

"I don't understand what you fellows are talking about. Take this (and he held up a table knife). You in France call it un couteau. You Germans call it ein Messer. We in England simply call it a knife which, all said and done, is precisely what it is."

Lord Coggan, M.A., D.D.,
Formerly the Archbishop of Canterbury, 1974-80.

The after-dinner speaker had been introduced in flattering terms. On rising to reply, he said:

"Such an introduction makes me pray two prayers for forgiveness: the first for my introducer, because he has told so many lies; second for myself, because I have enjoyed it so much."

Lord Caradon, G.C.M.G., K.C.V.O., P.C., O.B.E.,
Permanent U.K. Representative at the United Nations, 1964-70.

The local preacher in his prayer:

"Use me, Oh Lord, use me, even if it be only in an advisory capacity."

I first went to the United Nations as an Ambassador when my name was Hugh Foot and soon resigned because I disagreed with my Government on a question of African policy at that time.

A year or two later I returned to the United Nations as Permanent Representative of the United Kingdom and as a Minister of State having been sent to the House of Lords and having taken the title of Lord Caradon.

When I was speaking at a dinner in Chicago recently, the lady who introduced me had been one of the principal assistants and supporters of Adlai Stevenson when he was United States Ambassador to the United Nations. She said that she had known Hugh Foot as a close friend of Adlai Stevenson and she and he were sad when Hugh Foot left in disagreement with his Government on a point of principle, but some time afterwards she was sitting with Adlai in the General Assembly of the United Nations when the President of the Assembly called on the Permanent Representative of the United Kingdom, Lord Caradon, to address the Assembly.

And she looked, and said to Adlai:

"Funny thing, all these English look the same."

**The Late Sir Olaf Caroe, K.C.S.I., K.C.I.E., F.R.S.L.,
Governor, North-West Frontier, 1946-47.**

Vicereine of India (to A.D.C. at dinner party with music):

"Captain Mottram, do go and ask the bandmaster what is that charming tune!"

A.D.C. (in full regimentals) marches to band, makes enquiry, returns, and stands to attention before Vicereine, clinking spurs:

"I shall remember your kisses, Your Excellency, when you have forgotten my name!"

**The Late Sir Michael Cary, K.C.B.,
Formerly Permanent Under-Secretary of State, Ministry of Defence.**

The British Ambassador was in Washington some years back. About a fortnight before Christmas he was rung up by the local T.V. Station.

"Ambassador," said the caller, "What would you like for Christmas?"

"I shouldn't dream of accepting anything."

"Seriously, we would like to know and don't be stuffy. You have after all been very kind to us during the year."

"Oh well, if you absolutely insist, I would like a small box of crystallised fruits."

He thought no more about it until Christmas Eve when he switched on the T.V.

"We have had a little Christmas survey all of our own," said the announcer. "We asked three visiting Ambassadors what they would like for Christmas.

"The French Ambassador said: 'Peace on earth, a great interest in human literature and understanding, and an end to war and strife.'

"Then we asked the German Ambassador and he said: 'A great upsurge in international trade, ensuring growth and prosperity, particularly in the underdeveloped countries. That is what I wish for Christmas.'

"And then we asked the British Ambassador and he said he would like a small box of crystallised fruits."

Field Marshal Sir James Cassels, G.C.B., K.B.E., D.S.O.,
Chief of the General Staff, Ministry of Defence, 1965-68.

This is a story about a colonel of the Indian Army who, after 40 years' service in the East, retired to Scotland.

One day, he and an old friend set forth to have a "blood match" on the local golf course. The colonel took his fox terrier with him.

It was a cold, cold day and, when they had started, the colonel, due to his many years in the East, found that he had to retire frequently behind a tree, a whin-bush or a bunker.

Meanwhile, his terrier was roaming around too.

His Scottish caddie was entranced with this performance!

Eventually, at the 17th tee, the colonel drew his breath and said in a low voice:

"Caddie, what's the state of the game?"

The caddie, in a broad Scots accent, said:

"I couldna' say, Colonel, but ye're two up on the doggie."

Sir Hugh Casson, K.C.V.O., R.A., R.D.I.,
President of the Royal Academy.

A young man with expectations from an aunt, discovered she was a lover of Keats. He therefore bought a mynah bird, taught it to recite "Ode to a Grecian Urn", and sent it off to his aunt.

After some weeks he rang to enquire whether his aunt had received the bird.

"Yes," she said, "and it was delicious."

Two girls overheard on tube.

"I can't bear late nights. If I go out to dinner and am not in bed by twelve I go home."

Sir Richard Catling, C.M.G., O.B.E., K.P.M.,
Commissioner of Police, Kenya, Inspector-General, 1963-64.

Having bought a gun-dog and paid a good deal more for it than he had planned, or wished to pay, the dog's new owner was left with the uncomfortable and slightly guilty feeling which such circumstances inevitably provoke — that he had been less than sensible in his purchase, and perhaps even foolish. Nevertheless, being a keen wildfowler, it was not long before he visited a mere not far away from his home with the dog to try his luck with the morning flight. Not long after arriving there he was successful in shooting a duck which fell into the mere.

The new dog was told to fetch and straightway ran over the surface of the water, picked up the floating body of the duck, returned with it running over the top of the water and laid it at the feet of the wildfowler.

As daylight strengthened so did the tally of duck grow. All the birds fell into the mere when shot and all were retrieved by the dog running over the top of the water without even wetting its feet.

At the end of the shoot, and pondering on the dog's strange behaviour as he walked round the edge of the mere in the direction of the place at which he had left his car, the wildfowler came upon a solitary fisherman engaged in putting up his rod, little stool, umbrella and all the other impedimenta which the coarse fisherman seems to gather to himself with such eagerness. He stopped and the two men were passing the time of day when a lone duck happened to come over. Quickly reloading, the wildfowler brought it down and the bird fell into the middle of the mere.

Once again, when commanded, the dog ran out over the top of the water, retrieved the duck, brought it back and laid it at his master's feet.

Neither wildfowler nor fisherman spoke. But as the former ejected the spent cartridge from his gun, put the duck into his bag and prepared to go on his way he said rather shamefaced:

"I only bought this dog a couple of days ago and, as a matter of fact, I foolishly paid a good deal more for it than I had intended and can afford."

There was silence and then the fisherman replied:

"Whoever persuaded you into that deal pulled a fast one on you; the dog can't even swim."

Lance Cattermole, R.O.I.,
Painter and Illustrator.

A well-known artist was painting a very beautiful girl nude back view. One morning, after she had taken her stand on the dais, he suddenly put down his palette and brushes and protested:

"How often have I told you not to wear those tight girdles which leave marks on you! For heaven's sake go and sit down until they've disappeared!"

The girl duly complied, and after a wait of ten minutes began to pose again.

But the painter took one look at her, flung down his brushes and shouted:

"You would go and sit on the only cane-bottomed chair in the studio!"

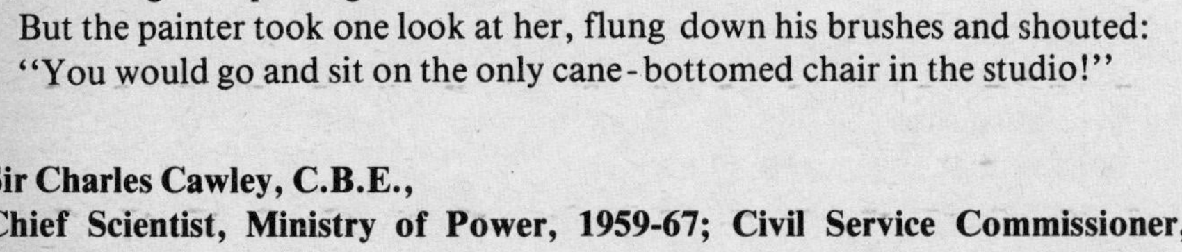

Sir Charles Cawley, C.B.E.,
Chief Scientist, Ministry of Power, 1959-67; Civil Service Commissioner, 1967-69.

James Thurber tells of a teacher who gave her pupils a book on penguins to read and asked them to write an essay on it. My heart goes out to the little girl whose essay consisted of a single sentence.

"This book," she wrote, "told me more about penguins than I wanted to know."

Will, aged seven years, had something of a reputation at school for not paying attention. He came home one day and proudly announced to his mother that the class had had a lecture from a visitor.

"What was it about?" asked his mother.

"I don't know," came the reply.

"Why, weren't you listening?"

Will was outraged.

"Of course I was listening," he said indignantly. "The man didn't tell us what it was about."

I fancy I have heard that lecture, too.

Lord Champion, P.C.,
Deputy Speaker and Deputy Chairman of Committees, House of Lords.

A little group of us were standing talking in a corridor of the House of Lords, when along came an old hereditary Peer who had recently married a young wife. We congratulated him. He thanked us and said:

"I must have an heir; I must have an heir."

As he tottered off down the corridor one of the group said:

"The old boy is certainly heir minded but I doubt if he's heir conditioned."

Sydney Chapman, R.I.B.A., F.R.T.P.I., M.P.,
Originator of National Tree Planting Year, 1973.

This story is true and actually told by me after my election defeat as Member of Parliament for Birmingham, Handsworth, at the February, 1974, General Election. The Lord Mayor was the Returning Officer announcing the result.

"Finally, my Lord Mayor, let me say that the main distinction I had in the last Parliament was to be the only architect in the House of Commons. Therefore I claim that I am the only failed politician tonight who can say with literal truth: 'Ah well, back to the drawing board'."

Viscount Charlemont,
Air Ministry Liaison Officer, 8th and 9th U.S. Army Air Force, 1942-45.

An Irishman from Co. Tyrone invited to a shoot in England was given a butt next to his host who took the end of the line.

The cry of "mark over" was followed by the sight of a cock pheasant flying directly along the line. Each gun in turn missed and in taking evasive action the old pheasant was quite a height by the time it came over the Irishman, whose shot brought the bird down with a tremendous crash.

"Oh! good shot, Murphy," called his host, "a remarkable shot."

To which his guest modestly replied:

"Sure it was nothing at all; the fall would have killed him anyway."

Air Marshal Sir Edward Chilton, K.B.E., C.B., F.R.I.N.,
Air Officer Commanding-in-Chief, R.A.F. Coastal Command, 1959-62.

To be immortal in speech is not to be unending.

Q.C. to Judge: "My Lord, I'm sorry, I appear to be running out of time."
Judge to Q.C.: "Mr. Smith, you have already run out of time; now you are trespassing upon Eternity!"

Lord Clifford of Chudleigh, O.B.E., D.L.,
Count of the Holy Roman Empire; Farmer and Landowner.

The cannibal's wife went to the cannibal butcher and said she wanted to give her husband a treat for the Sunday lunch.
"What," said the butcher "does he like?"
"He is particularly fond of brains. What have you?"
"We have Missionary's Brains at 30p a lb."
"I think we had that last time," said the wife.
"Well, we have Seaman's Brains at 35p a lb."
"I hear they are rather salty: have you any more?"
"Yes, we have House of Lords' Brains; but they are 90p a lb."
"This is scandalous," said the housewife. "30p and 35p yes, but 90p is ridiculous. I shall report you to the Prices and Incomes Board."
"Please, madam, don't," said the butcher. "You've no idea the number of Lords we had to kill to get a lb's worth of brains."

The Late Sir Andrew Clark, Bt., M.B.E., M.C., Q.C.,

My uncle, a country parson and a connoisseur of port, went to dine one night with his rural dean. The rural dean, though rich, was notorious for the inferior wines that he used to produce for visiting clergy. After dinner my uncle sniffed the port suspiciously and gingerly sipped it. A look of surprise came over his face and turning to his host he exclaimed:
"Henry, this is Cockburns 1908! Where on earth did you get it?"
To which the rural dean replied:
"My dear Alec, on the rare occasion when you produce a good sermon I don't ask you where you got it from."

Sir Eric Clayson, D.L., F.C.A.,
Chairman, Birmingham Post and Mail Group, 1957-74.

A speaker, proposing the toast of "The Guests" at the Annual Banquet of the Birmingham Chamber of Industry and Commerce some years ago, referred in his speech to the late Miss Edith Pitt, the first woman to represent the Edgbaston Constituency of Birmingham in the Commons.

He mentioned that it was perhaps not strictly correct to describe her as an M.P., since the dinner was taking place in the interregnum between the dissolution of Parliament and the forthcoming General Election, and she was therefore temporarily unseated.

"Hence," he added, "the origin of the expression 'the bottomless pit'."

Sir Joseph Cleary, J.P.,
Lord Mayor of Liverpool, 1949-50; Freeman, City of Liverpool, 1970.

Rejoinder to bombastic cleric interrupting a speaker:

"If the meek shall inherit the earth, you are bankrupt right now."

The late Robert Kennedy:

"Some men see things as they are and say 'Why'. I see things that never were and say 'Why not'."

George Clouston,
Formerly Musical Director, B.B.C.

Two Irishmen were working on a building site. The first Irishman, Pat, shouts to his companion Mick:

"Hey, watch out, Mick, the bricks are falling out of the wall."

Just then, a brick falls and hits Mick, taking off his ear. Mick falls to the ground bleeding profusely but Pat says:

"Take it easy, Mick, I'll find your ear and we'll take you to hospital, they'll soon sew it back on."

Pat searches amongst the rubble, finds Mick's ear and takes it over to where Mick is lying.

"O.K.," says Pat, "I've got it."
Mick looks at it:
"That's not mine, you bloody fool — mine had a cigarette behind it."

**Major-General Ronald Coaker, C.B., C.B.E., M.C., D.L.,
High Sheriff of Leicestershire.**

Behind every successful man there lies an ambitious wife — and an astonished mother-in-law.

**The Late Viscount Cobham, K.G., G.C.M.G., G.C.V.O., T.D.,
Governor-General of New Zealand, 1957-62; Lord Steward of the Household, 1967-72.**

The Governor of a far-off Colony somewhere in the tropical zone was reporting to The Queen on the state of affairs in his territory. His letter ended as follows:

"Your Majesty may be interested to learn that as I write the Residency is being besieged by a hostile mob some 400 strong. Should they succeed in breaching the outer defences of the Residency, my soldiers will withdraw from the courtyard and try and defend the main door of the building. Should they fail in their endeavours, it seems likely that I shall not much longer remain

"Your Majesty's most humble and obedient servant,
"John Brown, Governor."

**Sir Barnett Cocks, K.C.B., O.B.E.,
Clerk of the House of Commons, 1962-73.**

An American professor from the Middle West, over here to make a study of the British way of life, told an English friend that what impressed him most about us was our civic responsibility and support of law and order. Asked to elaborate, he said:

"Almost every time a serious crime is committed in your country, the newspapers report that a man is helping the police with their enquiries."

**Sir Jack Cohen, O.B.E., J.P.,
Mayor of Sunderland, 1949-50.**

Three Cambridge dons were walking by the river one beautiful hot summer day, and coming to a secluded spot could not resist the temptation to have a dip. Not having costumes with them they went in "in the buff". Unfortunately, just as they came out, a punt full of pretty female undergrads came round the bend, whereupon in some consternation two of the dons grabbed some clothes around their middles, whilst the third threw something over his head!

After the girls had gone, the two who had covered their middles turned on the other and said:

"Why on earth did you do that?"

Whereupon he answered:

"Where I come from we recognise people by their faces!"

**Rear-Admiral George Kempthorne Collett, C.B., D.S.C.,
Vice Naval Deputy, S.H.A.P.E., Paris, 1955-57.**

During both World Wars, the Fleet was stationed for long periods at Scapa Flow, which is not renowned for its bright lights or amusement facilities. One of the measures taken to provide recreation for the Fleet was the construction of a 14-hole golf course on the island of Flotta, and on Sunday afternoon, when the Fleet was in harbour, ships' boats full of golfers could be seen making their way across the harbour towards the first tee.

A certain Admiral, who had recently hoisted his Flag in the Fleet, was told that this was the normal routine on Sunday afternoons. He therefore sent for his Flag Lieutenant and told him that he would be required to play golf with his Admiral that afternoon.

There was quite a crowd of junior officers waiting to drive off at the first tee

when they arrived, but the Admiral was quickly recognised and teed his ball up without delay, hitting a beautiful shot right down the middle of the fairway.

The Flag Lieutenant then addressed his ball, and much to the amusement of the onlookers did a complete air shot. The midshipmen sniggered as he tried again, with similar results. After his third failure to make any connection with the ball, he looked up, smiled at his gallery and said:

"Damned difficult course, this."

Adrian Redman Collingwood, C.B.E., T.D.,
Chairman, Eggs Authority, 1971-78.

A young friend of mine went in for club car racing and for that purpose had a souped up old "Sunbeam".

At 3 a.m. one morning he was closely following a police car when suddenly a cat ran on to the road and the police driver jammed his brakes on. Inevitably my friend hit the police car and after what seemed an eternity a large policeman got out, looked at the "Sunbeam" and said:

"How do you stop that bloody thing when I'm not about?"

The Late Air Vice-Marshal Sir John Cordingley, K.C.B., K.C.V.O., C.B.E.,
Controller, Royal Air Force Benevolent Fund, 1947-62.

A distinguished French politician having celebrated his 90th birthday was asked by a friend:

"How do you find life now you are 90?"

"Fine when you consider the alternative."

A Member of Parliament in an after-dinner speech went on for an incredibly long time. When he finally sat down he said to his neighbour:

"How did that go?"

After thought, the neighbour replied:

"At least it will shorten this ruddy winter."

An old man was asked by a friend:

"What do you do now that you have retired?"

He replied:

"Myman brings me a cup of tea and a copy of 'The Times'. I drink the tea and read the obituaries and if I am not included therein I get up."

Sir Walter Coutts, G.C.M.G., M.B.E.,
Governor-General of Uganda, 1962-63; Director, The Farmington Trust.

In the days when it was possible to grant to your children property free of death duty provided the grantee lived for five years, an old farmer thus gave his farm to his two sons. One lovely June day, some three months before the appointed date, he passed quietly away in his chair. The sons were aghast but the younger and more intelligent said:

"Ah, we have a deep freeze."

So into the deep freeze the old man went. Come November they got him out, dusted him off, and put him in his chair. They rang up the doctor who came, pronounced a heart attack but said:

"I must make a post mortem first to make sure."

The sons were on tenterhooks.

Much later the doctor said:

"It was as I thought, but the one thing which puzzled me was that his stomach was full of fresh strawberries."

The younger and more intelligent of the two said:

"Ah! We have a deep freeze."

Lieut.-General Sir John Cowley, G.C., K.B.E., C.B.

Two young men were on a walking tour in Wales. They stayed one night at a lonely house, where they were offered a room each by the owner, a middle-aged woman living alone who was clearly doing her best to conceal her age.

Next morning they left after paying their bill.

Nine months later one of them received a solicitor's letter, which surprised him. He rang up his friend and the following conversation ensued:

"Do you remember the house we stayed in during our walking tour in Wales last year, where there was a blousy looking woman living alone?"

"Yes, I remember her well."

"Did you leave your room during the night and visit her room?"
"Yes, as a matter of fact, I did."
"Did you, by any chance, give her my name instead of yours?"
"Yes, I'm sorry about it, and I should have told you before — I hope nothing has gone wrong."
"That explains it. Today I received a solicitor's letter saying that she had died, and left me in her will £10,000."

The Late Sir Beresford Craddock,
Barrister; Member of Speaker's Panel of Chairmen, 1966-70.

Two elderly sisters were most devout and regular attenders at the kirk every Sunday morning. The minister was a fine God-fearing man whose only fault, if it is a fault, was that his sermons were never less than fifty minutes.

On one particular Sunday he excelled himself by continuing for over the hour, and was still going strong, when one of the sisters (very deaf) turned to the other and asked in a loud voice:

"Is he no feenished yet?"

To which the other replied:

"Aye, he's feenished, but he canna stop!"

Brigadier Sir Douglas Crawford, C.B., D.S.O., T.D.,
Lord Lieutenant, Metropolitan County of Merseyside, 1974-79.

At a crowded dinner party:

"Can you all hear me at the back of the room?"

A voice from the back of the room:

"Yes, I can hear you perfectly well, but I don't mind a bit changing with somebody who can't."

The Chinese have a succinct yet accurate method of description. They would say:

How pleasant it is to dine — with nice people.
How pleasant it is to wine — with nice people.
How pleasant it is to sleep (Pause) — with a contented mind.

Sir Robertson Crichton,
Judge of the High Court of Justice, Queen's Bench Division, 1967-77.

In September, 1939, my Brigade Headquarters, in which I held a post of, understandably, minor importance, received a Most Secret signal from the War Office — no less. It read:

"A Prisoner of War Camp is being established at Barnet. On no account is it to be publicly known that this is a Prisoner of War Camp. It will be referred to solely as 'Cockfosters Camp' and no reference will be made to the fact that it is a Prisoner of War Camp.

"Telegraphic address:
PRISWAR BARNET."

Sir Moore Crosthwaite, K.C.M.G.,
H.M. Ambassador to Sweden, 1963-66.

At the end of a St. Andrew's Day dinner, when all other honourable speakers had been called upon, someone asked for a speech from the young piper, who had been knocking back tumblers of whisky. Greying slightly, but maintaining the caution for which Scotland is famous, he said:

"Thank you very much. I've had a very good time so far."

Roland Culver, O.B.E.,
Actor.

There was a charity dinner which I attended and the opening speaker, who had dined and wined too well, proceeded to burble on for perhaps half an hour and bored the assembled company into a state of coma.

The next speaker rose and was merciless. This was his reply. Almost in a whisper he said:

"Mr. Chairman, My Lords, Ladies and Gentlemen.
Replying to Sir Richard Lumber
I'm loth to rouse you from your slumber
since brevity is the soul of wit
my kindest act must be to sit."

And sit he did.

**The Late the Hon. Geoffrey Cunliffe,
Deputy President, British Standards Institution, 1964-70.**

A company of which I was chairman was giving a staff dinner. The managing director, who was presiding, stood up without warning and said:

"I will now ask Mrs. Cunliffe to say grace."

I was sitting next to her and she whispered:

"Tell me what to say."

I said, "I'll whisper and you repeat it after — For what we are about to receive (repeated loud and clear) — may the Lord give us tolerance and true understanding (repeated loud and clear)".

It wasn't till a little sudden laughter erupted that she realised what she had said.

Admiral Sir Angus Cunninghame Graham of Gartmore, K.B.E., C.B., J.P., Flag Officer Scotland, 1950-51.

An old farmer, Elder of the Kirk, was heard muttering as he left the General Assembly of the Church of Scotland after one of its periodic verbal storms:

"Meenisters are like manure — benifeecial when spread o'er the land, but kind o' nauseous when in a heap."

**Sir James Currie, K.B.E., C.M.G.,
Community Relations Commission; in H.M. Diplomatic Service until 1967.**

The head of an Oxbridge College was for some time in hospital. The governing body met in his absence and decided to send him a telegram.

It read: "Governing body met today, and wish you a speedy recovery by 18 votes to 17."

Don't forget Sydney Smith:

"Serenely full, the epicure would say
Fate cannot harm me, I have dined today."

Vice-Admiral Sir John Cuthbert, K.B.E., C.B., Flag Officer Scotland, 1956-58.

The other morning in our water meadows, I heard two of our cows talking.

One said to the other:

"Daisy, you're not looking very well this morning, are you feeling all right?"

Daisy replied:

"No, I'm not — in fact I'm feeling awful. The trouble is that I went to several parties last night — the first was with the Guernseys, then on to the Red Polls and finishing with the Aberdeen Angus. Anyhow, I didn't wake up this morning, I missed being milked — and now I've got a hell of a hang-under."

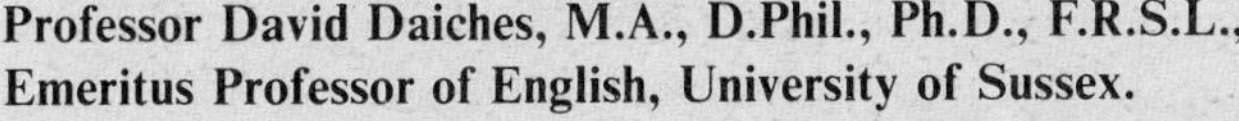

Professor David Daiches, M.A., D.Phil., Ph.D., F.R.S.L., Emeritus Professor of English, University of Sussex.

A New York gentleman buttered a piece of toast during breakfast, then accidentally dropped it on the floor. He bent down to pick it up, and saw to his astonishment that it had landed buttered side up, which he knew from experience was against all the laws of nature. Buttered bread or toast always fell buttered side down. He was so puzzled by what happened that he went to see his rabbi (he was Jewish) to whom he explained what had happened.

"How can you explain such an astonishing and unnatural event?" he asked.

The rabbi pondered a while, then told the gentleman he would have to consult various authorities before he could give a definite reply. So would the gentleman please come back in a week's time.

The following week the gentleman returned.

"Well, rabbi," he said, "have you found the explanation of that extraordinary matter of the buttered toast?"

"Well," the rabbi replied, "I have consulted many books and talked with many colleagues. It seems that there is only one possible explanation. You must have buttered the toast on the wrong side."

Dr. Lionel Dakers, F.R.C.O., A.D.C.M., F.R.A.M., F.R.S.C.M.,
Director, Royal School of Church Music.

During my fifteen years as organist of Exeter Cathedral, my neighbour was Bishop Westall, at that time Bishop of Crediton. Renowned as a high churchman, he was in the habit of driving around the diocese wearing his purple cassock and biretta. One dark and stormy evening, while on his way to a confirmation somewhere on Dartmoor, his car died on him. After a while, a lorry appeared on the lonely road. Seeing the bishop in trouble, the driver volunteered to take him to the nearest garage.

Eyeing the bishop up and down, the driver commented:

"Lummy, guv'nor — what a night to be going to a fancy dress party."

Pierre Monteux, the famous conductor, was reputed to have been interviewed on the B.B.C. on his 90th birthday. Asked what his pleasures in life were at the age of 90, this alert Frenchman replied:

"I still have two abiding passions; one is my model railway, the other — women. But — at the age of 90, I find I am getting just a little too old for model railways."

Tam Dalyell, M.P.,
P.P.S. to the Late R.H.S. Crossman, 1963-70; Vice-Chairman, Parliamentary Labour Party, 1974-76; Member of European Parliament, 1975-79.

A doctor, an architect and a politician argued as to whose was the oldest profession.

"Obviously, the medical profession is the oldest," said the doctor, "since the first doctor was the one who took the rib out of Adam to create Eve."

The architect disagreed.

"The first architect created order out of chaos in the firmament, so mine must be the oldest profession."

"Ah!" said the politician, "but it was the first politician who created the chaos."

The Late Rt. Hon. Sir Harold Danckwerts, A Lord Justice of Appeal, 1961-69.

I was sitting in the Court of Appeal with Ben Ormerod, L.J., and another L.J.

A powerful looking woman appeared before us. She wanted leave to appeal out of time against a decree of divorce which her husband had obtained against her on the ground of cruelty.

While Ben Ormerod was discussing the matter with her, I was looking through the shorthand notes of the evidence and I discovered that she had hit her husband on the head with a shovel, so I said to the woman:

"Mrs. — , what about this incident with the shovel?"

"Oh," she said, "that was merely love play."

Major Lord Darling of Langham, D.L., Deputy Lieutenant of Somerset, 1972, Avon, 1974; Chief Executive of the Royal Bath and West and Southern Counties Society, 1961-79.

Some years ago I was motoring in the Irish Free State. I was stopped by a policeman who asked if I was after knowing that I was in a 30 m.p.h. limit. I said I did not know any such thing, but he said to be sure I was and that I was travelling at forty miles an oor. He said he would be after seeing me loicence so I gave it to him. Whilst he was reading it very slowly I had a quick think.

"I must get to the other side of Ireland today," says I.

"I'm after reading your loicence," says he.

"Well," says I, "so that we can settle the matter do you have anything like summary fines over here?"

"No," says he, "it usually rains."

Sir Charles Davis, C.B.,
Second Counsel to the Speaker, House of Commons, since 1974.

A Flemish intellectual is sitting on a park bench in Brussels, when a Walloon joins him and starts chatting to him in Flemish. Soon they are joined on the bench by a Jesuit priest and Father Christmas. Then a pretty girl walks by, and one of the men winks at her. Which one was it?

It must have been the priest, because all the other characters are imaginary.

Colonel D.J. Dean, V.C., O.B.E., T.D., D.L., J.P.,
Deputy Lieutenant of Kent, 1957.

When a young lieutenant was promoted to captain, by error the date in the "Gazette" appeared as April 1st, 1041, instead of 1941.

That evening, after celebrating his promotion in the Mess with his fellow officers, they persuaded him to apply for back pay and allowances. The application was correctly made out, quoting Pay Warrant and King's Regulations, and was posted. Then all retired to bed.

Next morning the young officer realised with horror what he had done and was filled with trepidation as to the outcome. A Court Martial?

Weeks later the Paymaster replied:

"Your application for pay and allowances dating back to April 1st, 1041 has been found to be in order and your account has accordingly been credited with £39,999. You appear however to have overlooked a paragraph in King's Regulations under which a Commanding Officer is personally responsible for any guns or horses lost in action owing to negligence. If the C.O. is killed his responsibility devolves upon the next senior surviving officer. Your letter proves conclusively that you are the sole survivor of the Battle of Hastings (1066 A.D.) where 20,000 horses valued at £2 each were lost by negligence. The responsibility for £40,000 therefore falls upon you. I have accordingly adjusted your account to the extent of a net debit of £1."

"What kind of sport has our distinguished guest had?" Lord Minto, one-time Viceroy of India, asked the native bearer, who had attended an American guest.

"Oh," replied the Indian, "the young sahib shot divinely but Allah was merciful to the birds."

Lord Delfont,
Chairman and Chief Executive of Trusthouse Forte Leisure Ltd.

The scene is a monastery where every seven years a monk is selected to pass an opinion of life within the community.

At one of the seven-year meetings, the Abbot calls upon Brother Albert to say what he feels, and the privileged monk asks:

"Why is our soup always cold?"

Seven years later, Brother John is invited to speak, and he says:

"The soup is not always cold but is sometimes hot."

Another seven years pass and this time Brother Richard is called upon. He says:

"I want to resign the Order."

When asked why, he contends:

"I'm sick and tired of this constant bickering."

Sir Lionel Denny, G.B.E., M.C.,
Lord Mayor of London, 1965-66.

A nonconformist minister who had preached vigorously all his life against the wickedness of betting found himself in Ireland and was tempted to attend a race meeting, to see for himself what went on. Not surprisingly he saw one, if not more, Catholic priests there and he actually saw one bless a horse about to run in a race.

He remembered the number of the horse, which won the race. His curiosity roused further he continued to watch the priest, whom he saw bless, respectively, two more horses who also won their races.

By then, completely demoralised, the minister convinced himself that there was no chance about the outcome and after seeing a horse for the fourth race being blessed he hastily placed all his money upon it. The race started but before very long the horse began to falter and finally dropped down dead.

Distraught, the minister sought out the priest and told him his unhappy experience.

The Catholic was distressed and said:

"You must be a Protestant!"

"Indeed I am," said the nonconformist.

The other replied:

"Sure then you would not be knowing the difference between a blessing and giving the last rites!!"

**Lord Deramore,
Chartered Architect.**

A civil service mandarin spent part of his retirement pension on the purchase of a shooting estate in Scotland and told the factor he required a privy to be built for the convenience of his guests.

Ever practical, the man asked:

"Would you be wanting a single-seater or a two-seater, so I can get enough timber?"

"I'll let you know about that later, Angus."

"And where would you be thinking of having it?"

"Eh? Well, I'll have to consider that and inform you."

Some months later the factor asked whether the mandarin had come to any decision and received the reply:

"Don't bother me now, Angus. I've got more important things to deal with."

Still more months passed before the civil servant summoned the factor to his presence and announced:

"Angus, I've been thinking about that privy . . . . "

"Och, man," interrupted that worthy, "I've built it already!"

"The devil you have! And where did you put it?"

The factor described its location, which appeared to have no snags as far as his employer could see, so he thought for a moment and then asked:

"Is it a single-seater or a two-seater that you've built?"

"Och, I made it a single seater, 'cos I ken you'd never make up yer mind which hole to sit on."

The Duke of Devonshire, P.C., M.C.,
Chancellor of the University of Manchester.

I was sitting next to a very distinguished man at a large public dinner at which I was about to speak; my neighbour was not on the list of speakers, and I turned to him and said:

"Oh how I hate having to make a speech."

To which he replied, fixing me with steely look:

"Oh do you, I don't mind a bit, I just can't bear listening."

Peter Dimmock, C.V.O., O.B.E.,
Director, American Broadcasting Co. Worldwide T.V. Sports Syndication.

A small and weedy man arrived at a lumberjack camp in the northern forests of Canada. As all the men working at the lumberjack camp were at least six feet tall and big husky men at that, they simply couldn't believe that the new arrival was in fact a lumberjack. They therefore gave him a very small axe and took him to a small sapling. The man duly spat on each palm and with two flicks of his wrists chopped the sapling down.

The big husky lumberjacks immediately thought that he was taking the mickey and so decided to teach him a lesson. They gave him one of the largest and heaviest axes that they could find and took him to a particularly tall and thick tree.

"Go on, cut this down," they said.

"All right," he replied.

Again he spat on his palms, picked up the axe and was just about to hit the tree when he turned to them and said:

"But you have not given me the line."

Whereupon the lumberjacks thought, "He evidently does know a bit about it," and so they pointed to another tall tree on the horizon.

Within a very few minutes the new arrival had sent the big tree crashing down absolutely straight on the line that he had been given.

"Amazing," said the lumberjacks, "but how on earth is it that someone as small and weedy looking as you can fell trees so well; where exactly do you come from?"

"The Sahara," he replied.

"But there are no trees in the Sahara," said one of the lumberjacks.

"Not any more," replied the new arrival.

The Late Sir Philip Dingle, C.B.E.,
Town Clerk of Manchester, 1944-66.

The late Lord Birkett was a member of the Saints and Sinners Club; on one occasion he was due to propose the health of the late Nye Bevan at a dinner of the club at which Nye Bevan was to be the guest of honour; the day before the dinner was to be held came and he had not thought of anything suitable even though he stayed up till a very late hour; then he remembered that his father had frequently told him that when he was in a difficulty he should take a "sors Biblicae", so he got out his Bible and let it fall open and let his fingers alight where chance determined; the passage on which his finger fell read:

" . . . . and they tried to get nigh unto Jesus but they could not for the press".

(This was told to me by Lord Birkett himself but he added, "Don't waste your time trying to find it because it is not in the Bible".)

Sir Douglas Dodds-Parker, M.A.,
Member British Parliamentary Delegation to European Parliament, 1973-75.

Groucho Marx taking Harpo's pulse and remarking:

"Either he is dead or my watch has stopped."

Sam Goldwyn, when being reminded that "You can't take it with you," replied:

"Then I will not go."

The Rt. Hon. Sir John Donaldson,
High Court Judge; President National Industrial Relations Court, 1971-74.

A political judge is unknown in Britain. A British judge's attitude towards politics is like that of a monk towards sex:

A frank admission of the fascination of the subject; nostalgic recollections of youthful indiscretion; a nagging feeling that he might do better than the practitioners, but a stark acceptance of the fact that it is not for him.

The Suffragan Bishop of Dorking
(The Rt. Rev. Kenneth Dawson Evans).

It is said that Frederick Temple, Archbishop of Canterbury eighty years ago, was much feared. This was particularly the case when he entertained at his house those who were about to be ordained. It was the interview that they feared.

He said to one young man who was to be ordained deacon on the following day.

"I will lie on the couch, as if I were ill. Go out, come in again and 'sick-visit' me."

The young man went out, knocked at the door, walked up to the Most Reverend, Frederick, Lord Archbishop of Canterbury, looked at him with a serious air, waggled his finger and said:

"Freddie, you're on the drink again!"

Robert Dougall, M.B.E.,
Freelance Broadcaster, Television and Radio; Author; President, Royal Society Protection of Birds, 1970-75.

An American is on his first visit to Scotland.

At breakfast he finds his host seated before a plate of porridge. He watches fascinated; then asks:

"Are you going to *have* that?"

There is a pregnant pause and then the American is struck by an awful thought. He adds in awesome tones:

"Or have you *had* it?"

Judge John F. Drabble, Q.C.,
A Circuit Judge, 1965-73.

A man told his friend he knew a joke which would make him die of laughing. The friend insisted upon hearing the joke, laughed and laughed until he died. The police did not believe the joker's explanation and charged him with murder.

At the trial the accused was made to recount the story and the jury laughed and laughed and died.

The judge adjourned the case.

Two days later, walking to Court, the judge suddenly stopped. And he laughed and laughed until he died.

Judge The Lord Dunboyne.

Greater love hath no man than this — that he giveth away his best after-dinner story to charity:

A schoolmaster who tried to teach me divinity went on holiday in the Holy Land, and took a trip on the Sea of Galilee for which he was in his view overcharged. He paid . . . and, as an afterthought, gently remarked:

"No wonder Jesus walked."

Sir Kingsley Dunham, F.R.S.,
Foreign Secretary, The Royal Society, 1971-76; Former Director, Institute of Geological Sciences.

I was at the Chicago World's Fair of 1933 as a young man. Finding a stand making phonograph recordings, I decided to send one to my fiancée (now Lady Dunham) and went into the studio to dictate a long message in what were, to say the least, very endearing terms.

Looking through the glass windows I noticed a small crowd had gathered outside.

When I went out, armed with my record, I found out why; the whole proceedings had been relayed on powerful loudspeakers.

"My," someone remarked, "it sure was nice to hear a genuine English voice."

The Bishop of Durham
(The Rt. Rev. John Stapylton Habgood, M.A., Ph.D.).

The young ordinand, who was being sent as curate to a country parish, was worried by his lack of experience in country matters. He therefore decided that perhaps he could make a start by teaching himself how to milk a cow.

Seizing a bucket and stool, he approached a likely looking cow in the middle of a field and set to work. The cow had other ideas, and moved off across the field; whereupon the young man picked up his bucket and stool and started again. Once more the cow moved off and the young man with it.

When this had happened several times, a friend who was watching from the road shouted to the ordinand:

"What are you doing?"

Back came the reply:

"About three miles to the gallon."

Sir Esmond Durlacher,
Member of The Stock Exchange, 1926-77.

Amongst the majority of the racing public it has always been the view that the chief obstacle to their making money is the bookmaker. He pinches the odds and whatever happens, he always manages to make a profit.

In the City, those who deal in stocks and shares — the speculators, the stockbrokers, the investment managers of the insurance companies, the pension funds, the unit trusts, etc. etc. — also hold very much the same view of the stock-jobbers! In fact, this has been so since Samuel Johnson described the stock-jobbing fraternity as "an unnecessary collection of low fellows who speculate in the 'Funds' and are of no benefit to anyone but themselves".

Wherefore the following story with the knowledge of the foregoing factors mentioned in this prologue is, I think, a good example of the ready wit of the members of the Stock Exchange.

One morning I was sitting at my desk when a friend — a member — rang me up and said he was sorry to hear our office had been burgled overnight, but had I heard the story (9.30 a.m.) already circulating on the floor of the House. When I said:

"No, I have not," he replied:

"It is understood that the burglars were very lucky and got away with only a small loss!!"

(And we had in fact been burgled!)

The Late Sir Cyril Dyson,
President of the National Association of Goldsmiths in Great Britain and Ireland, 1957-70.

I was asked to present the prizes at a girls' school. It is always difficult to think of something to say other than, "Congratulations", "Well done", etc.

The girls came up in age groups and eventually the head girl came up to collect the several prizes she had won. She was a nice looking girl of about 17. I wondered what I could say to her. Suddenly I thought that as this was her last term it would be appropriate to ask her:

"And what are you going to do when you leave school?"

She looked at me very coyly and said:

"Well I *had* thought of going straight home."

Sir John Eardley-Wilmot, Bt., M.V.O., D.S.C.,
On the Staff of the Monopolies Commission.

A British Diplomat was asking Mao Tse-tung some questions after having been granted a rare interview.

"What do you think would have happened if Mr. Khrushchev had been assassinated instead of President Kennedy?"

Chairman Mao thought and then said:

"I don't think Mr. Onassis would have married Mrs. Khrushchev."

Earl Fortescue,
Landowner; Late Coldstream Guards.

How do elephants make love under water?

They first remove their trunks.

Judge T. Elder-Jones,
A Circuit Judge, formerly Judge of County Courts.

An Anglican vicar noticed that an Evangelical neighbour was having some success with posters displaying slogans exhorting this and that, and decided to follow suit.

After much thought he devised a winner:

"IF YOU'RE TIRED OF SIN STEP IN."

Imagine the poor man's chagrin when the next day he saw written below his text:

"BUT IF YOU ARE NOT, 'PHONE PADDINGTON 04655."

Air Marshal Sir Thomas Elmhirst, K.B.E., C.B., A.F.C.,
Lieutenant-Governor and Commander-in-Chief of Guernsey, 1953-58.

Scene: The small mail steamer from Glasgow on its route up the West coast of Scotland.

On the bridge the captain and a couple of lady schoolteachers he had invited up there.

A heavy shower of rain approaches. Captain in a loud voice down the

"voice-pipe" to the saloon below where one of his crew is in charge of the bar:

"Is there a big mackintosh down there that would cover two ladies?"

Reply, by a small man in the corner, after a moment's silence:

"Noo, but there is a wee MacGregor here that is prepared to try."

George Elrick, F.R.S.A.,
Former President of the Entertainments Agents Association.

Two sailors were going home on leave after a rough time in the Cod War. Arriving at Invergordon to go on their leave they got into a train and found themselves sharing a compartment with a parson.

After the train moved off a little, one sailor says to the other:

"What are you going to do with your leave, Jack?"

"I am going to get drunk on beer every night. That's my hobby. How about you?"

The other sailor says:

"Girls are my hobby. I am going to see a different one every night and have a marvellous time."

The train moves on. One sailor looks at the paper and on reading it says to his friend:

"What's lumbago, Jack?"

"I don't know — ask the parson," was the reply.

So the sailor says:

"What's lumbago, sir?"

As the parson was annoyed at the way they had been talking, he replied:

"Lumbago, my man, is a very painful disease, due to drinking beer and going out with women. Why do you ask?"

"It's nothing, guv'nor — it just says in the paper here that the Bishop of London has got it."

Sir John Elstub, C.B.E.,
Industrialist and Company Director.

Here is a true story about a visit to Russia, and the moral is always take your own interpreter — because the official one provided will almost certainly give a somewhat watered-down version of what was actually said.

We were visiting metal factories and were accompanied by a Mr. B., from the ministry concerned.

One factory manager, in the course of polite small-talk, said:

"Mr. B. who is with you is a very eminent metallurgist in our country. A few years ago he won the Stalin Prize for Metallurgy."

Mr. B. then replied in Russian and we got two nearly simultaneous translations.

The local guide said:

"Mr. B. said that because he won the Stalin Prize, he had had no unfair promotion."

Our interpreter then chipped in to say that what he had really said was:

"And a fat lot of bloody good that did me!"

Sir Basil Engholm, K.C.B.,
Permanent Secretary, Ministry of Agriculture and Fisheries, 1968-72.

A duke, living on his country estate, used to have his breakfast in bed every Sunday morning. One Sunday there was a knock at the door and a new very pretty young girl brought in his breakfast, and put it down on the bedside table.

"You're new, my dear," said the duke. "And where might you be from?"

"From the village, sir," she said.

"Come and talk to me, my dear," said the duke.

"Yes, sir," said the girl.

"You know, you're very pretty dear. Come and sit down on the bed," said the duke, patting a place near him.

"Yes, sir," said the girl and came and sat down.

"You know my dear, you must learn the right way to address me. You should say 'Your Grace'."

And the girl fell on her knees beside the bed, and said:

"For what I am about to receive, may the Lord make me truly thankful."

Lord Erskine of Rerrick, G.B.E., K.St.J., F.R.S.E., Hon. F.R.C.P.E., D.L., J.P.,
Governor of Northern Ireland, 1964-68.

Incident narrated to me by the late Rt. Hon. Thomas Johnston, C.H., which came to his knowledge while he was Regional Commissioner for Scotland during the war.

Air-raid warden on his rounds in a populous and dark area of Glasgow observed a light which he went to investigate. The following conversation took place between him and a small boy who answered his knock on the door.

Warden: "Is your father in?"

Boy: "No, my father went oot when my mither came in."

Warden: "Is your mother in?"

Boy: "No, my mither went oot when my brither came in."

Warden: "Is your brother in?"

Boy: "No, my brither went oot when I came in."

Warden: "Then are you in charge of the house?"

Boy: "It's no a hoose, it's a lavatory!"

Sir George Erskine, C.B.E., Director, Morgan Grenfell & Co., 1945-67; President, Institute of Bankers, 1954-56; High Sheriff of Surrey, 1963-64.

Australian on his cattle station when asked by a Scotsman if there were many Scottish people in Australia answered:

"Yes, a good many but our real plague is rabbits."

Sir Francis Evans, G.B.E., K.C.M.G., D.L.,
Agent for the Government of Northern Ireland in Great Britain, 1962-66.

Very soon after entering the foreign service in 1920 I was sent by my then chief, the Consul-General at New York, to represent him at a public dinner. I found myself seated next to a distinguished old American gentleman with white hair and a neat white beard, charming and gracious to a very young man.

After a little conversation he said to me:

"Were you at Oxford, Mr. Evans?" I replied in the negative.

He asked "Cambridge?" and again I said "No".

His next question was:

"What was your university?"

My reply was that I had missed university owing to the War, having gone straight to the Army from school.

He said:

"How very interesting! I did the same; I missed university for exactly the same reason. The War, you know."

I did what is known transatlantically as a "double take" at the white beard and other indications of at least fifty years' difference in age, whereat he explained with lifted forefinger:

"Ah, but I mean the Civil War."

He was Major George Haven Putnam, founder of the famous publishing house of G.P. Putnam's Sons. He had been wounded and taken prisoner by the Confederates at an early battle in the War of the States.

Lieut.-General Sir Geoffrey Evans, K.B.E., C.B., D.S.O.,
General Officer Commanding-in-Chief, Northern Command, 1953-57.

A certain organisation required a replacement for one of their top officials who was shortly to reach the age of retirement. The post, a highly paid one, called for exceptional qualifications and accordingly an advertisement, setting out the conditions, was inserted in the press.

Sometime later the board met to consider the applications and to prepare a short list for interview, and among the applicants appeared the name of a Mr. A. His age and his qualifications exactly fitted the company's requirements and the chairman was delighted. In fact he suggested that they need hardly look further.

However, one of the members interrupted and said:

"I do not know Mr. A. personally but I have heard that he is inclined to lift his elbow to a startling degree and I feel we should proceed with caution."

Following some discussion and in view of A's high qualifications, it was decided to include him in the short list and at the same time to find out whether his drinking habits were as bad as they were alleged to be.

So, on the appointed day when those on the short list were assembled and Mr. A. was ushered into the board room, the chairman opened by saying:

"Good morning, Mr. A. Please sit down. Do smoke if you wish."

There followed a series of technical questions on the conclusion of which, the chairman said:

"Now, Mr. A., the board would like to ask you certain questions of a different nature and the first is — supposing the word 'Haig' was mentioned to you, what would it remind you of?"

Without hesitation Mr. A. replied:

"I would immediately recall that famous Commander-in-Chief, Earl Haig, who led the British Forces to victory in France, in the First World War."

"Thank you," remarked the chairman. "But supposing I said 'White Horse' — what then?"

"Ah," retorted Mr. A., "I would remember the pleasant days I have spent in the Vale of the White Horse in the beautiful English countryside in spring and summer."

"Now, one last question," continued the chairman, "What are your immediate reactions to the words VAT 69?"

Mr. A. looked puzzled and, after a moment's thought, replied:

"Gentlemen, I fear you have me beaten there. Could it possibly be the Pope's telephone number?"

**Major-General Sir Robert Ewbank, K.B.E., C.B., D.S.O.,
Commandant, Royal Military College of Science, 1961-64.**

A friend once introduced me as "This Battle-Scared Warrior".

Realising his mistake, he hastily corrected himself: "I....I...mean This Bottle-Scarred Warrior!"

The missionary met a man-eating lion in the bush. He fell on his knees and buried his face in his hands. Peeping through his fingers, he saw the man-eater on its knees in front of him, paws in eyes.

Unable to bear it longer, the missionary shouted:

"I'm praying to be delivered from the jaws of the lion. What on earth are you doing?"

The lion growled back:

"I'm saying grace!"

The Late Professor Sir Alexander Ewing, M.A., Ph.D., LL.D.,
Professor and Director of the Department of Audiology and Education of the Deaf, University of Manchester, 1944-64.

Samuel Alexander, O.M., our Manchester Professor of Philosophy, 1893-1924, was invited by a Liverpool shipowner to dine and stay overnight. He arrived at his host's house on his famous bicycle — his favourite means of transport.

Before dinner-time the shipowner's valet came to him with a hurried message:

"Sir, the Professor does not seem to have brought any evening clothes."

"Then I won't change for dinner myself," was the reply.

Very soon, however, the valet hurried in with another message:

"Sir, I have just seen Professor Alexander going downstairs in a dinner jacket."

"Get mine out for me quickly," said his master.

Later came another discreet message from the valet:

"Sir, the Professor has no pyjamas with him."

"Put a pair of mine out for him," he was told.

Next morning, when replacing these pyjamas, unused, the valet remarked:

"The Professor had his own, after all."

When the time came for the Professor's departure, his bicycle was brought round and his host accompanied him to the door, to see him off.

"Have you no luggage?" he asked curiously.

"I'm wearing it," the Professor replied.

Lord Fairfax of Cameron,
Lawyer.

An Irish priest, teaching his class divinity, offered a shilling to the boy who could name the greatest man in history.

"George Washington," said one.

"Christopher Columbus," said another.

"St. Patrick," shouted a little Jewish boy.

The priest gave the Jewish boy the shilling and asked:

"Why did you say St. Patrick?"

"Well," replied the Jewish boy, "Of course I know the real answer is Moses — but business is business."

Sir James Falconer, M.B.E.,
Town Clerk of Glasgow, 1965-75.

The Environmental Health Officer was investigating a report about vibration being felt on the top flat of a multi-storey block. His first reaction was that there was no evidence to support the complaint. The woman of the house explained however that the trouble was at its worst when she was lying in bed and a double-decker bus passed. She invited the inspector to lie on the bed and experience the vibration for himself.

No sooner had he done so than the husband came in. The inspector's embarrassment prompted the immediate explanation:

"I doubt if you are going to believe me, mister, but I'm just waiting for a bus."

The Late Lord Feather, C.B.E.,
General Secretary, Trades Union Congress, 1969-73.

A big local authority in the North had received a bequest of a large estate including a mansion house and a lake. The council had already decided that the mansion would be a museum and art gallery and the lake would be a pleasure area and have a boat-house.

An independent councillor moved that the council should purchase a gondola for the lake. A member of the ruling party immediately moved an amendment that they should buy two, breed from them and sell the progeny to other authorities and thus be self-supporting.

The Lord Mayor, appalled at the ignorance of his colleagues, said: "Please withdraw your amendment — don't you know that a gondola is a cheese!"

Lord Ferrier, E.D., D.L.,
Late Chairman of Companies in India and the U.K.; Hon. A.D.C. to Governor of Bombay.

A friend of mine was travelling in the train and opposite him sat a gentleman reading "The Times". Every now and then he took a complete sheet of the newspaper, crumpled it up, opened the window, threw it out and shut the window.

After he had done this two or three times my friend said: "Excuse me, sir, but I am most interested in what you are doing. May I ask why you do it?"

"Oh yes," he replied, "it keeps the elephants away."

"But," my friend said, "there aren't any elephants here."

"Of course not," came the answer. "That proves it works!"

Professor David John Finney, C.B.E., F.R.S., F.R.S.E., M.A., Sc.D.,
Professor of Statistics, University of Edinburgh.

Some years ago, I took my two younger children to an evening for children at the Harvard University Observatory. Of course the sky was cloudy, and except for a brief glimpse of the moon the telescopes could give no satisfaction. We were then assembled in a lecture room, perhaps 200 in all — more than half children, and these mostly under 10 and all looking highly intelligent. A young astronomer gave an excellent talk on "The Sizes of Heavenly Bodies", well illustrated with the aid of an enormous balloon. Around me I could see notes being made by tiny hands with small pencils and scraps of paper.

After about 40 minutes, the lecturer stopped and rashly invited questions.

Behind me a little 7-year-old voice piped up; reading from his carefully prepared paper, he asked — with a clarity that could well be imitated by older questioners at scientific or political meetings:

"Will the lecturer please tell us how far it is from the Earth to the planet Mercury?"

The lecturer was a cautious scientist, unwilling to risk an approximate truth.

"It depends," he said, "on the time."

Back came the small boy:

"Well, say at 6.30."

Viscount FitzHarris.

When asked which piece of the salmon he would prefer, the local farmer replied:

"The tail end, starting from just behind the ears."

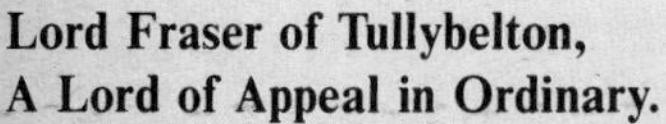

Lord Fraser of Tullybelton,
A Lord of Appeal in Ordinary.

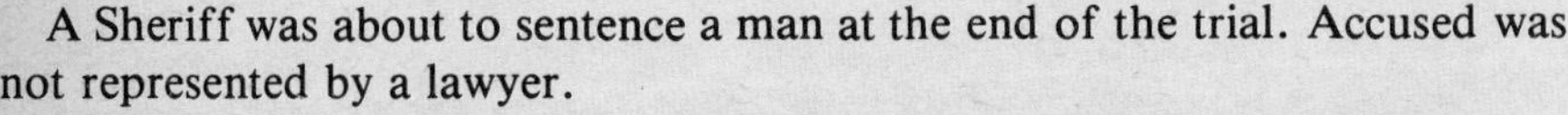

A Sheriff was about to sentence a man at the end of the trial. Accused was not represented by a lawyer.

The Sheriff asked whether the man had anything to say before sentence.

The accused muttered:

"Damn all."

The Sheriff leaned over to the clerk and asked:

"Did the accused say something?"

Clerk: "He said 'Damn all', my lord."

"That's funny, I could have sworn I saw his lips move," said the Sheriff.

The Rt. Hon. Sir Geoffrey de Freitas, K.C.M.G., M.P.,
Vice-President of the European Parliament, 1975-79.

The old lady was dying. Her husband was by her bedside. Her chief joy in life had been cooking him each morning a good breakfast.

"When I am gone, John," she said, "you will marry again soon, won't you, so that you can get a good breakfast in the mornings."

"My dear," said her husband, "don't talk of such things. I am not thinking of marrying again."

"But, John, I won't go happy unless you find another wife soon. She can have everything of mine except my clothes. Remember that, John, not my clothes."

"It's all right, my dear," said John, "they wouldn't fit her."

Air Vice-Marshal Edward Frith, C.B.,
Senior Administrator, University of London.

A guardsman was about to retire from the Army after a period of long, devoted and loyal service. His commanding officer, at the interview given prior to retirement, asked the guardsman if there was anything he could do for him on his return to civilian life.

"Yes, sir," came the quick reply, "I would like to take my rifle with me on retirement; it has seen me through thick and thin, I rescued it from Dunkirk, I have stood with it for hours and hours outside Buckingham Palace and it has been at my side on endless guard duties. I have cleaned and polished it for days and I have marched with it on my shoulder over distances longer than I care to remember. The rifle is now obsolete anyway and I would be ever-indebted to you if you could grant this one request on my retirement."

The commanding officer pondered and eventually said:

"Yes, I can understand your attachment and sentiment — take the rifle with you."

The guardsman was last seen in the barracks marching away, in a smart manner, with the rifle on his shoulder.

He had not been idle during the twilight of his career and had prepared his house and garden prior to retirement; in fact, his lawn was immaculate — his pride and joy. He was next seen, to the utter amazement and consternation of his wife, digging up his magnificent lawn and laying down a mass of concrete. By this time, his wife was beside herself.

He made a plinth and duly mounted the rifle on it. He then stood back, admired his handiwork and exclaimed:

"Now rust, you bastard, rust!"

Sir Geoffrey Furlonge, K.B.E., C.M.G.,
Author; H.M. Ambassador to Ethiopia 1956-59.

An Ambassador once travelled from Paris to Istanbul on the Orient Express, and was bitten by bugs on the way. He sent a strong complaint to the company, and in reply received a letter stating that they were horrified that so eminent a person should have suffered in this way; that such a thing had never in their experience happened before; that they were taking stringent measures to prevent any possibility of a recurrence; and that they begged him to accept their humblest apologies.

All very proper. But unhappily the clerk who dealt with the complaint, by inadvertence, attached to this reply the Ambassador's original letter of complaint, across which someone had scribbled:

"Usual bug letter please."

Air Vice-Marshal Jack Furner, C.B.E., D.F.C., A.F.C., F.I.P.M.,
Assistant Air Secretary, Ministry of Defence (Air), 1973-75.

The really significant difference between the various nationalities is the way they react to a funny story.

When you tell an Englishman a funny story he laughs three times — the first time when you tell it to him, the second time when you explain it to him, and the third time when he catches on.

A Russian on the other hand only laughs twice — the first time when you tell it to him, the second time when you explain it to him — he never catches on.

A German will laugh just once because he catches on straight away.

And an American doesn't laugh at all because he's heard it before.

Air Vice-Marshal Maxwell Gardham, C.B., C.B.E.,
Registrar, Ashridge College, Berkhamsted.

The four old gentlemen of the city made it a practice to walk across the city park in the long summer evenings, chatting of art, literature and music. They were the Leader of the City Silver Band, the City Librarian, the City Baker and a very old and revered Professor of English.

They all enjoyed these excursions, and were so engaged one long summer evening when they came across four young ladies of obvious easy virtue sitting on a park bench; the four ladies wished the old gentlemen "Good evening", and wondered if they might be of service. Graciously the old gentlemen refused the offer and continued their walk in deep thought.

After a while a voice said:

"Do you know, I've never seen *four* of those together before, I've seen them singly, of course, but one wonders, what would be the collective noun for a body such as that?"

The City Baker thought that the collective noun was a JAM of tarts.

The Leader of the City Silver Bank inclined toward a FLOURISH of strumpets.

After much thought the City Librarian said that they were a VOLUME — of trollopes.

The old Professor of English, however, walked on ahead shaking his white mane.

"You are all quite wrong, quite wrong. They are neither a *Jam*, nor a *Flourish* nor a *Volume*."

"What then, Professor?"

"Undoubtedly the collective noun for a body such as that would be an ANTHOLOGY."

"An anthology, Professor?"

"Yes. An Anthology of English Prose."

Lord Gardiner, C.H., P.C.,
Lord High Chancellor of Great Britain, 1964-70; Chancellor, The Open University, 1973-78.

I was sorry for the man in the dock at the Old Bailey. He was a "Con" man and he had gone to some trouble, in a period of imprisonment, to think out his next get-rich-quick scheme. He eventually acquired a small bookshop from which he made a very modest income. He became, however, very well to do because he read the obituaries in "The Times" and whenever a clergyman died he sent in an account "To Account Rendered" for £29.4.6d, or some modest amount. (It is extraordinary how many clergymen die.)

Almost inevitably he received a cheque in settlement. Sometimes if the executor was a difficult solicitor or chartered accountant they wrote and asked for a copy of the account. He would then send them a copy of the full account containing "The Sexual Life of Greece and Rome", "Lady Chatterley's Lover", etc., and then they paid very quickly.

After a few years he had some very bad luck; the solicitor to the executors was a tiresome man and the deceased had been blind for nine years.

Lord Garner, G.C.M.G.,
Chairman, Commonwealth Scholarship Commission in the U.K., 1968-77.

When I am introduced with undue emphasis as a pillar of the Establishment I find it salutary to recall the entry under my name in "Who's Who" for 1966, at a time when the Nuclear Disarmament Campaign provoked great controversy.

After listing my position as Head of the Diplomatic Service and P.U.S. at the Commonwealth Office, it described my recreations as "All anti-war activities".

My staff were aghast; I was furious at the implication that I was working against the policies of the Government I had the honour to serve.

I protested indignantly but received a gentle explanation. I, having thought "skiing" was somewhat pretentious for my then advanced years, had made a MS. alteration in the handwriting that I myself generally find so easy to decipher: this had read "all out-door activities"!

Sir Peter Garran, K.C.M.G.,
H.M. Ambassador to the Netherlands, 1964-70.

A poor old widow woman in Australia was one day invited to come to a solicitor's office to be told that a distant relative in England had died and left her a lot of money. The dear old thing was quite overcome; what was she going

to do with all that money at her age?

"Well," suggested the solicitor, "what about making a trip to England to see the old country for yourself?"

"What, me?" said the old woman. "Me go to that country where all those convicts came from?"

Lord Geddes of Epsom, C.B.E.,
President of the Trades Union Congress, 1954-55.

If in an argument you preface your response with "With respect", you really mean that the argument put forward is a little silly.

If you preface it with "With great respect", you really mean the argument is very silly.

If you preface it with "With very great respect", you really mean that it is "b......... ridiculous!"

Peter W. Gibbings,
Chairman of The Guardian and Manchester Evening News Ltd.

In the Senior Common Room, the members of an Oxford College were considering in what to invest some college funds.

The Bursar recommended land.

"Land," he said, "has proved a very good investment for the last one thousand years."

There was a murmur of approval from his colleagues except for the history don.

"That's all very well," said he, "but you must remember the last thousand years have been quite exceptional."

Sir Derek Gilbey, Bt.,
Retired Wine Merchant.

An English golfer playing at Muirfield for the first time with a very dour Scottish caddie arrived at the third hole and after a good drive asked his caddie what club to take.

"You'll be wanting your spoon," was the laconic reply.

"I don't like the lie much," said the Englishman, "I think I'll try my 3 iron."

He was handed it without a word and made a wonderful shot pitching just short of the green and then running into the hole.

"How about that?" he said, turning to the caddie.

"Aye, it was a good shot but ye'd have done better with yer spoon."

Professor Iain E. Gillespie, M.D., M.Sc., F.R.C.S.,
Professor of Surgery, University of Manchester.

Jock McTavish couldn't sleep. He twisted and turned so much that his wife Jean asked him what was the matter.

"Ah'm worried," he said. "You see, six months ago I borrowed £50 from Angus McFlannel across the road, and I cannot pay it back. Ah've no idea how I'll raise the money, and I'm so worried about it."

On hearing this, Jean got promptly out of bed, went over to the window, opened it wide and yelled across the street:

"Hey, Maggie — Maggie McFlannel!"

Eventually a sleepy female head in curlers appeared at a window directly opposite and yelled back:

"What is it?"

Jean went on:

"My Jock owes your Angus £50 and he canna pay it back."

Whereupon she slammed the window shut again, got back into bed, turned to her husband and said:

"Now he's worrying about it. There's no need for you to worry any more. Get back to sleep."

Colonel Sir John Gilmour, Bt., D.S.O., T.D., J.P.,
Lord Lieutenant of Fife; Member of Parliament for East Fife, 1961-79.

The Moderator of the Church of Scotland and the Archbishop of Canterbury agreed to have a meeting in order to discuss the ecumenical movement.

The Moderator suggested that the meeting should be held at Scotch Corner, as although it meant travelling to England to meet the Archbishop, it gave the appearance of meeting on Scottish ground.

They agreed to meet at 12 o'clock and both duly arrived at the same time, but due to thick fog, had a head-on collision in the car park. The Moderator climbed out of his Mini and assisted the Archbishop, who was very shaken, out of his Rolls-Royce.

The Moderator, seeing this, took out his flask and offered the Archbishop a dram, which he took with gratitude.

The Archbishop then reached for his flask and offered a return dram to the Moderator, who replied he would sooner wait until after the Police had arrived.

Lord Gisborough, D.L.,
Landowner and Farmer.

A young man bought a new fast car and tried it out on a nearly straight road in Ireland where he lived.

He accelerated to 60, 70, 80, and realised the straight yet narrow road went over a hill top. But there was never any traffic so he topped the rise at 100. Standing on the road talking were two Irishmen with a tractor. The car swerved to the left, over the fence, over the field, through the next fence and shuddered to a halt.

One Irishman turned to the other and said:

"Begorahh Paddy, we just got out of that field in time."

The Bishop of Gloucester
(The Rt. Rev. John Yates, M.A.).

A Very Important Person was aggravated by what he considered to be incompetent service from the new steward at his club.

"Do you know who I am?" he thundered.

"No, sir," was the reply, "but I will make enquiries and then come and tell you."

Sir Colin Goad, K.C.M.G.,
Secretary-General, Inter-Governmental Maritime Consultative Organisation, 1968-73.

The master of a ship was observed, each time she put to sea, to go to the safe, unlock it, extract a large black book, read carefully, replace it in the safe and lock up.

The other officers were most curious but could never get hold of the old man's keys.

One day the master died and was buried at sea in the customary way, but the chief officer had taken care to get hold of the keys.

Eagerly the safe was unlocked, the book extracted and opened.

There was a single entry:

"Port is on the left; Starboard on the right."

Lord Adam Gordon, K.C.V.O., M.B.E.,
Comptroller to Her Majesty Queen Elizabeth The Queen Mother, 1953-73.

An after-dinner speaker as he was ending his speech said:

"And now I feel like Lady Godiva, who as she approached the end of her ride through Coventry said to herself — thank goodness I'm nearing my close."

Major-General R. Gordon-Finlayson, O.B.E., J.P., D.L.,
President of Nottingham Royal British Legion, 1971-79; High Sheriff of Nottinghamshire, 1974.

On a long wartime rail journey in U.K., the U.S. G.I. took a 1st class ticket, only to find all seats taken and he had to stand in the corridor.

On walking along the train, he found a dog sitting on one seat. Inquiry to its lady owner simply produced:

"I have paid for Fifi's ticket, so Fifi sits in a seat."

At intervals, this same conversation is repeated, until the G.I. was so infuriated he seized the dog and threw it out of the window. Whereupon one of the other U.K. passengers remarked:

"You Americans do everything wrong; you drive on the right; you eat dinner at 6 p.m.; you think we British despise you; and now you've thrown the wrong bitch out of the window."

Lord Gore-Booth of Maltby, G.C.M.G., K.C.V.O.,
Head of Diplomatic Service, 1968-69; Chairman, Save the Children Fund, 1970-76.

Once upon a time, a quarter of a century ago, there lived in Washington, U.S.A., a newspaper columnist called George Dixon. To be met with in any choice bar, he had a round (not fat) body, close-cropped hair, a round face, round horn-rimmed glasses and a hearty greeting for everybody. This was combined with a profound mistrust of all people of intellectual or social pretensions like democratic politicians or Britishers generally. Here is one of his anecdotes, not, regrettably, in his own words except for the last line which is genuine.

At a marble-topped table in an old-fashioned café there sat a somewhat gloomy man sipping intermittently from a glass. There were other such tables around, one very much in a corner.

Looking up from his glass, the gloomy man pointed to the corner table and said firmly:

"Waiter, there's a pigeon under that table."

"But, sir, this restaurant is fully screened, every precaution is taken . . ."
"There is a pigeon under that table."
After more such argument, the waiter and a colleague dragged away the heavy table with difficulty from the corner.
"Yes, sir," said the pigeon, "any messages?"

The Late Captain Lord Alastair Graham,
Late Royal Navy; Farmer; Former Alderman, East Suffolk County Council.

A young mother (let us call her "Susan") was as most mothers are, inordinately proud of her first baby, so when Susan's mother came to stay she suggested that the old lady might like to see baby have its bath. Having done so Susan asked her mother what she thought of the baby.
"Oh, I think it's a splendid child," she replied, "but tell me is it a boy or a girl?"
"Have you lost or mislaid your spectacles?" said Susan.
"No, darling, but I've lost my memory!"

Sir Arthur Grattan-Bellew, C.M.G., Q.C.,
Chief Secretary, Tanganyika, 1956-59.

A golfer was bending down with his back to the tee, looking for his ball in the rough, when a lady drove off the tee and her ball hit him, a perfect bull's eye.
He picked up her ball and walked back to the tee and said:
"Madam, the hole you should be aiming for has a flag in it!"

Lord Greenwood of Rossendale, P.C., D.L.,
Minister of Housing and Local Government, 1966-70; Pro-Chancellor, University of Lancaster, 1972-78.

A parliamentary candidate was touring an office which was computerised. He suggested that they should ask the machine what the result of the election would be. Back came the reply:
"It says that *you* will win, but that personally it would not vote for you."

Joseph Greig,
Actor.

This is a report that appeared in "The Shetland Times" many years ago; a newspaper, still going strong, which was co-founded by my grandfather just over 100 years ago.

"During the funeral procession of Mr. William Johnson, who died at the age of 79, his boyhood friend John Jamieson, aged 77, dropped dead at the graveside. Naturally this threw a gloom over the entire proceedings."

The Late Lord Grenfell, C.B.E., T.D.,
Deputy Chairman of Committees, House of Lords.

After riding a gallop on my horse, one of the trainer's grooms came in on foot and stated:

"I am terribly sorry, he fell dead. He has never done that before."

The Late Sir Kenneth Grubb, K.C.M.G.,
Chairman, House of Laity, Church Assembly, 1959-70.

My best after-dinner story was provided 50 years ago by an old Amazonian Indian (Amerindian). After a forest feast, when they had discussed whether to kill me, he said (I translate):

"I am not in favour; the last time we killed a white man, not a mouthful was given to me."

The Bishop of Guildford
(The Rt. Rev. David Alan Brown, B.A., B.D., M.Th.).

I was on trek in the South of the Sudan and spending the night at a small village school which was also a church centre. I was given the schoolroom as a rest-house and put my camp bed, with mosquito net, where there was an open space, along the wall opposite to the doorway. The classroom had neither doors nor windows, but simply gaps in the mud-block walls where they should have been. My young servant helped me put up my bed and sort out a few things; as he did so, he ventured the remark that Europeans were brave to sleep in such places; Africans preferred to sleep in small huts with closed doors and almost no windows, because they were better protection against lions and leopards.

After sunset I took a saucepan of sweet tea to the teacher's homestead and we sat round the fire for a while under the stars talking. Two African pastors were with me and our conversation turned to animal stories. They told of a family who had once lived nearby and of the pit full of snakes which they kept to send out on errands against their enemies. They told also of men who could turn themselves into lions and back again at will. The senior pastor claimed to have experienced this years before when walking to school at the beginning of one term. His companion on the two hundred mile journey had boasted he was a lion-child and when the pastor, then a schoolboy, had expressed disbelief, he had told him to go half a mile down the forest track and then look back. His companion meanwhile went into the forest by the roadside, and when the pastor looked back at the appointed place he saw a lion in the road staring after him. He ran down the road and when later his companion rejoined him, he simply asked him:

"Do you believe now?"

When at last I went to bed I began to think my classroom not so secure as it had seemed at first. Although I was travelling by lorry I had my bicycle with me, and I placed this across the door-space. I thought that if a lion came in it would at least knock the bicycle over and wake me up. It was a moonlit night and when I woke up after my first sleep, there in the doorway stood a great lion, its head stretched out and tail erect. I turned to the wall and prayed, not knowing what else to do, for my African friends were all asleep inside the huts which were some distance away.

When at last I plucked up courage to look again at the doorway, it was my bicycle that I saw sideways on, its shape was very like a lion's. It is surprising what fantasies fear can evoke.

The Earl of Haddington, K.T., M.C., T.D., F.R.S.E., F.S.A.Scot., Chairman of Trustees, National Museum of Antiquities, Scotland; Trustee, National Library of Scotland.

Every Saturday the minister played a round of golf with old Jock, the bell ringer, and always with the same result, for Jock never failed to win. So in despair the minister said one day:

"It's no use, Jock, going on, for it seems I'll never beat ye."

"Ah," said Jock, "but ye'll likely score over me yet, for the day may come when ye'll be standing at my grave to bury me."

"Aye," said the minister, "and even that will be your hole."

General Sir John Hackett, G.C.B., C.B.E., D.S.O., M.C., Principal of King's College, London, 1968-75.

There is, after all, something to be said for censorship.

When Dr. Bowdler set out in the last century so to adjust the text of Shakespeare that no line of the Bard's would ever bring a blush to even the most delicately nurtured cheek, he furnished Othello with a far, far better reason for strangling Desdemona than anything Shakespeare thought up for himself.

What, as justifiable grounds for homicide, can go further than the noble line:

"She played the trumpet in my bed."?

Earl Haig, O.B.E., D.L., F.R.S.A., Artist; Chairman, British Legion, Scotland, 1962-65; Member of the Royal Fine Art Commission of Scotland, 1958-61, and of the Scottish Arts Council, 1959-66; Trustee, National Gallery of Scotland, 1971-73.

My story describes the departure of the Prominente, a group of British officer prisoners-of-war who had connections with distinguished British personalities and were therefore being treated by Hitler as hostages, from Colditz. The order for removal was sent to us from Himmler, whose plan was to move us southwards for a last stand at Berchtesgaden.

We had little alternative but to comply with the German order. The senior British officer, Colonel Todd, had done his best to help us by threatening the Commandant with dire punishment after the war if he handed us over in violation of the Geneva Convention, which stipulated that we be given twenty-four hours' notice and be told our destination. The Commandant had merely replied that as the S.S. were in the neighbourhood he would be coerced into carrying out his order if he tried to evade it. Colonel Todd had offered to let us lie up, hoping that we would not be found before the Americans' arrival. We had decided not to hide, since it would have brought reprisals on the heads of the other prisoners, reprisals which might well have been in the form of shooting, because the Germans were desperate.

Just before midnight another Prominente, John Winant, son of the American Ambassador in London, was added to our group. Then General Bor Komorowski and the other Poles, John Winant and the other Prominente were all taken outside, where we had to listen to an official order being read out by one of the German officers. Then we walked slowly across the dimly lit courtyard from whose windows craned the heads of our fellow prisoners. With the sound of their cheers and encouragement to support us, we passed through the archway to find a double line of German soldiers who formed a passage leading to two buses, and were driven off with two outriders on motor-bikes in front and an armoured car behind. The clock struck midnight as we drove through the town.

It was now Friday, 13th April, 1945.

We were ignorant of the strategic designs of the super-power in whose name some minion at O.K.W. was moving our bus from Colditz southwards—just as he probably was ignorant of the speed with which the Third Reich was about to collapse. Perhaps I should not use the word "minion", since telegrams and orders from O.K.W. were said to be signed by Himmler in the name of Adolf Hitler himself, who had some special intention for us. Even though he knew the game was lost, he was determined to move us like pawns across the map of Germany. Hitler was in Berlin. The head of the dragon was about to be cut off by the two armies advancing from east and west. The swift closing of the pincers at a point on the Elbe to the north of us was to precipitate Hitler's death and to save us.

We in a later epoch have pictures in our minds of what happened to the Jewish hostages at the Olympic Games in Munich. We saw photographs of them being driven off by bus, and they, just as we did, looked apathetic in a mood of numb desolation. We had no knowledge of the wider spectrum as we were driven off through the night. We did not know of the jaws of the trap which were about to snap together separating Berlin from the armies in the south. We did not realise that Hitler was about to die after handing over the reins of government to Admiral Doenitz. Even so, it was a near thing. Hitler is said to have ordered our execution during his last days in the Bunker.

Our bus took us through Dresden — through what remained of Dresden after the raid. We drove through endless wastes of empty ruins looking eerie in the moonlight, after some time stopped on the outskirts near a public park. Here a lit-up tram full of workers went past us towards the city — the only sign of humanity we had so far seen. Our journey continued for about thirty miles till we began to climb upwards.

Then, when the bus could go no further, we got out, and as we did so we saw towering above us a fortress like Edinburgh Castle but on a higher rock. Our tortuous climb took us along a path, through an outer gate of the castle wall, through a tunnel, up a wooden ramp to a great archway. Here we paused, and then entering a small door at the side found ourselves climbing steps which led us finally to the top of the rock. We came out on to a great wide terrace, from which a vast panorama was visible in the early morning light.

We were in the fortress of Königstein.

Archibald Richard Burdon Haldane, C.B.E., D.Litt.,
Author; Trustee, National Library of Scotland.

A sleeping-car passenger on the night train from Euston to the North sent for the attendant before the train started and explained that it was essential for him to leave the train at Carlisle in the early hours to catch a connection to Dumfries. He explained that he was a heavy sleeper and always reluctant to get up, but stressed the necessity of his leaving the train at Carlisle. The attendant promised to see that the passenger's instructions were obeyed and that the latter could rely on him.

Next morning the passenger awoke to find the train just coming in to Glasgow.

In a fury he rang for the attendant and cursed and swore soundly at him for not putting him off at Carlisle. The attendant listened in silence.

"Man," he said at length, "Ye're a bonny sweirer, but ye're nothing to the man I pit oot at Carlisle."

The Late Sir John Hall, O.B.E., T.D., M.P., Chairman of the Select Committee on Nationalised Industries, 1972-74.

Not many in the House of Commons are worth painting, but some might be better for whitewashing.

The danger of political jokes is that they are sometimes elected.

Professor Peter Hall, M.A., Ph.D., F.R.G.S., Professor of Geography, University of Reading.

This is a New York Jewish psychoanalytic joke told to me by a member of the Ford Foundation. It made me laugh, but all academics laugh very loudly at jokes made by officials of the Ford Foundation.

Mr. Finkelstein went to consult Dr. Applebaum, the well-known psychoanalyst.

"What seems to be your problem, Mr. Finkelstein?"

"My problem is, doctor, I can't get on with my wife any more. Relations between us are a terrible mess. We've talked about a divorce. But before that I thought I should see if you can help."

"Well, Mr. Finkelstein," said the great Dr. Applebaum, "this is a commoner problem than you'd think. And it proves a real headache to cure. But just lately we've had some interesting reports coming through in the literature. They say that often, the real problem is just physical. Truth is, you may be physically run down and you may be worrying about that, so your marriage is going to bits. I can't say that it's the explanation with you, but at least it's worth a try.

"So here's what you should do. I want you to get out of bed tomorrow, get into a track suit, and do a real hard piece of jogging. Exactly ten miles, no more no less. Then the next day exactly the same. Keep it up for one week exactly, ten miles a day. You'll feel pretty terrible because you're badly out of shape. But persevere, and after a week call me to tell me how things work out."

"Doctor, it's worth a trial. I'll do just what you say."

A week later the 'phone rang in Dr. Applebaum's office.

"Hello, doctor, this is Mr. Finkelstein calling to say I did exactly what you told me. Ten miles a day. It was really tough but I made it and I'm beginning to feel really a lot fitter."

"Great! That's really fantastic. And now the $64,000 question; how are things with you and your wife?"

"How the hell should I know? I'm seventy miles from home."

Sir Richard Hamilton, Bt., M.A.,
Landowner; Playwright and Translator; Member of the General Council of the Tennis and Rackets Association.

A conference of Presbyterian ministers was taking place in a large country house in Scotland. The participants were allowed one free afternoon to themselves, but unfortunately the heavens opened to celebrate the occasion, to the accompaniment of a howling gale.

Nothing daunted, however, a gallant party of ministers opted for fresh air and exercise and decided to walk round the estate. They eventually found themselves approaching a decidedly rickety looking footbridge, and were wondering whether it would be safe for them to cross the seething torrent beneath when a highly excitable old gillie was seen running towards them making furious gestures.

The spokesman for the party, supposing that they were being challenged as trespassers, sought to reassure him.

"It's all right, my man," he said, "we're Presbyterian ministers from the conference."

"I dinna care whether ye be Presbyterians or noo," came the reply, "but if ye go over yon bridge, ye'll a' be Baptists!"

Lord Hankey, K.C.M.G., K.C.V.O.,
H.M. Ambassador to Sweden, 1954-60.

M. Talleyrand, Napoleon's Foreign Secretary, was talking to Madame de Staël, the famous intellectual, and Madame Récamier, the well-known beauty. Mme. de Staël felt he was paying too much attention to Mme. Récamier. So she said:

"M. Talleyrand, if you and I and Mme. Récamier were all shipwrecked together, and you could only save one of us, which would you save?"

M. Talleyrand replied with a bow:

"Madame de Staël, you know everything, so clearly you know how to swim."

John Hannam, M.P.,
Member of Parliament for Exeter.

An English Archbishop making his first official visit to the U.S.A. was duly warned of the dangers of being misquoted by the tough press reporters of that country. So he was determined to guard his tongue and when upon arrival at New York Airport he was presented to the throng of reporters in the V.I.P. room, he braced himself for the first question. This came from a tough Brooklyn-speaking reporter, who asked if the Archbishop intended to visit any of the famous New York clubs with their strip tease dancers.

The Archbishop thought carefully for a moment and replied with a little smile:

"Are there any such clubs in New York?"

Everyone laughed and applauded, and he was still congratulating himself upon his clever reply the next morning when the newspapers were delivered.

There, staring from the headlines was the bold caption:

Limey Bishop's First Question: "Are there any strip tease clubs in New York?"

Air Chief Marshal Sir Donald Hardman, G.B.E., K.C.B., D.F.C.,
Member of Air Council, 1954-58.

The executive was rather gloomy when he got to the office one morning, so his secretary asked him if anything was the matter.

"Nothing really," he said, "but it's my birthday and no one seems to have remembered it."

The secretary sympathised and after a while came back and said:

"Would you like to have a small party with me tonight?"

The executive looked at her and said he would very much like to.

"All right. Come to my flat at about 10 o'clock."

He turned up at the flat on time and was duly admitted by his secretary, looking ravishing, who ushered him in, gave him a drink, and asked him to sit down while she slipped into the next room. After what seemed an age to him she said through the door:

"Nearly ready — just another minute."

Then after a while:

"You can come in now."

He opened the door, and there was a wonderful sight. All his staff were there round a table loaded with food and champagne.

The only trouble was that by this time he had only got his socks on.

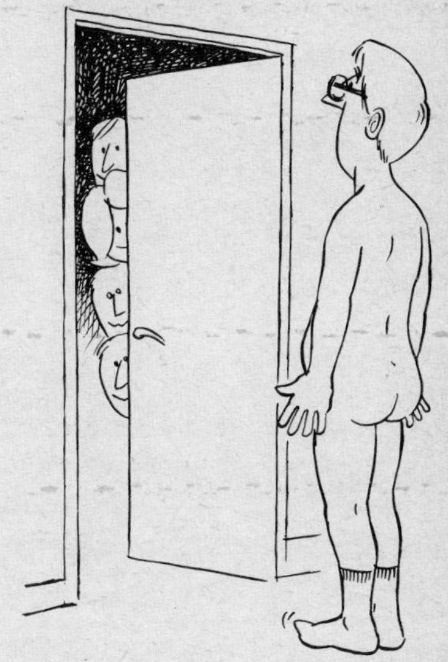

Sir James Harford, K.B.E., C.M.G.,
Governor and Commander-in-Chief, St. Helena, 1954-58.

A man told his trouble to the psychiatrist.

"Doctor, I don't know what's wrong with me. I say something, and a minute later I don't remember what I've said."

"Oh, that's interesting," said the doctor. "How long have you been like this?"

The man looked at him: "How long have I been like *what*?"

Lord Harris, C.B.E., M.C., D.L., J.P., Vice-Lieutenant of Kent, 1948-72.

A certain farmer, not renowned for his generosity, gave to one of his men during harvest time a glass of beer.

The man drank it but said nothing; the farmer asked him if it was all right.

He replied:

"Just."

The farmer asked him what he meant.

He replied:

"If it had been any better you wouldn't have given it to me; if it had been any worse, I couldn't have drunk it."

Rex Harris, Author and Broadcaster.

A large crowd was gathered before the gates of heaven.

Suddenly St. Peter appeared, and motioning the people to silence, he announced:

"Welcome to heaven, but before you go in, there are one or two things I want to tell you about God. . . firstly, she's black."

Robert Harris, Stage, Film and Television Actor and Broadcaster.

At an official banquet a friend was down to speak fourth.

The first three speakers had delivered themselves at great length. Finally an anxious toastmaster announced, with a slip of the tongue:

"My Lords, Ladies and Gentlemen pray for the silence of Mr. So-and-So."

My friend was quick to take his cue:

"My Lords, Ladies and Gentlemen" — a fractional pause — "Your prayers have been answered."

And sat down.

Sir William Harris, O.B.E., J.P.,
Surveyor and Company Director; High Sheriff of Greater London, 1971-72.

So often one hears today that "lack of communication" is the cause of lack of understanding between those "in authority" and those subject to such authority, e.g. the clergy have nothing in common with those to whom they preach — politicians nothing in common with those whom they represent — judges and magistrates nothing in common with those whom they punish.

In the latter category, at least, I think that I can claim to be the exception that proves the rule.

I received a telephone call one day from the deputy governor of a prison where I was a visiting magistrate stating that one of the prisoners had a complaint to make and insisted on seeing me. I duly visited the prison and listened to the complaint which the prisoner was making on behalf of himself and several others. I told him that whilst I considered the complaint to be serious and justified, I could not understand why he could not have waited until the next regular call of the visiting magistrate nor why he had insisted upon seeing me in particular.

He replied that he had discussed the matter with his fellow prisoners and they all felt that the complaint should be made to me personally. I said that this was what I could not understand — why to me?

To this question he replied, in all seriousness, that they all took the view that their complaint would receive much greater consideration from me because, he said, "we all think you are so much like one of us".

I like to think that this was meant as a tribute. Or was it?

Sidney Harrison,
Concert Pianist.

When television was a new toy the viewing public looked at simply everything. And they looked at me when I gave the first piano lessons ever given on television, and continued to look at a series of other programmes that I gave on the subject of serious music.

It was a new sort of experience for a good many people, and I soon learned that their relationship to me was oddly personal. What they said to me in the street was nothing like what I might hear in the artists' room after giving, say, a Chopin recital to a music society.

There was the man on the top of the bus.

"When are we goin' to see you again on the telly?"

I told him that, as I had just finished a series, the B.B.C. might decide that that was enough for the time being.

"That's right, guv'nor: never want to flog a dead 'orse."

Then there was the rave notice — if I may call it that — bestowed on me by the man who worked the curtain and the lights in a provincial concert hall.

"First time I saw one of your programmes I said to me wife, 'Christ, I can't stand much of this bloody lark,' but you sort of grew on me."

More seriously there was that time in Sydney, Australia, where a man ran after me in the street. He grasped me by both hands and told me that he had come to Australia as a refugee, how Australia had saved his life.

"But last night you talked to me about Beethoven and — you know — I am from Vienna . . . ." And suddenly he broke down and stood there in the Australian sunshine weeping.

However, to come back home, there was the shopkeeper who recognised me across the counter.

"Of course, you know what my wife thinks about you."

"Well, what does she think?"

He hesitated and then decided to continue.

"She says to me 'I don't know if I like that man by the looks of him, but he's got a lovely touch'."

Professor Ronald James Harrison-Church, B.Sc., Ph.D.,
Professor of Geography, London School of Economics.

During my first visit to Senegal in 1950 I had the good fortune to meet the captain of a French naval surveying sloop. He was a man of many interests, not least in archaeology which he practised successfully ashore, whilst his stories included one of the best I have ever heard.

He recounted how, after French West Africa transferred its allegiance from Vichy to the Allies, it was decided to send the battleship "Richelieu" from Dakar to the United States for refit, since it had not been to sea for some 2½ years, and to have its armament changed to take American ammunition.

So that it could make the transatlantic voyage, the French were asked by the Americans to prepare a list of needs for the voyage. One of the vital ones was for 1,500 new life-jackets (*brassières de sauvetage*), since the existing ones, then customarily stuffed with kapok, were unusable.

When the telegram containing this and other items arrived at the U.S. base the American authorities, knowing little or no French, were mystified at the request for 1,500 *brassières de sauvetage*, obviously thinking that meant female bras. So a cable was sent to the French asking if they really needed 1,500 *brassières de sauvetage*. The French, not realising the Americans might have misunderstood, confirmed they most certainly did.

My captain was in charge of the naval squad detailed to unpack all the American supplies. When they came to the *brassières* they were found to be feminine bras of all kinds, shapes and sizes. Naval discipline was extremely difficult to maintain. More seriously, the "Richelieu" soon after had to cross the then U-boat infested Atlantic without any life-jackets.

Fortunately, neither was the "Richelieu" sunk nor were the bras wasted, despite the French Navy then having no equivalent of the WRNS.

The bras were divided into two lots, and put in naval stores at Toulon and the other not inappropriately named base of Brest.

When, after the war, courtesy cruises were resumed, the stocks were drawn on for prizes at dances aboard large French ships when visiting foreign ports.

I went to a conference in the United States in deep summer 1952, not expecting to be there in the Fall. However, I was asked to lecture at a university, and during my return the weather was already quite cold. A woman professor welcomed me at Buffalo, and noticed I had only a raincoat. She explained that her husband had died a few months before, that he was of the same height and build as I, and that his coat, which she had had cleaned for disposal to charity, might fit me. It did, and I agreed to hand it in to a charity in New York.

However, it was so cold there that I kept the coat and, on arrival in England, wrote to her to ask what I should do, especially as I liked the coat so much and would like to keep it. However, exchange control then prevented the easy transfer of sterling into dollars, and their transmission to the American charity, so that it was agreed that I should give the sterling equivalent of the coat to a British organisation.

Unfortunately, I did not then know so much about Oxfam, but the Salvation Army benefited instead!

The Earl of Harrowby.

Toast used for the Ladies:
"Oh, the goodness of their goodness when they're good,
and the sadness of their sadness when they're sad,
but the goodness of their goodness
and the sadness of their sadness
is as nothing to their badness when they're bad."

Tramp seen on the road-side with a lighted match running down the seams of his shirt.

Passer-by: "What are you doing?"

Tramp: "Toasting the Visitors."

Frank Thomas Hart, J.P.,
House Governor and Secretary to the Board, Charing Cross Hospital, 1952-73; Hospital Administrator, Zambia Medical Aid Society, 1973-75.

A young police constable, giving evidence in a magistrate's court for the first time was very nervous.

The case was of a "lady" charged with indecent behaviour and offensive language. The Chairman of the Bench, a woman, asked the policeman what the defendant said.

He replied: "I don't think I can mention this in open Court, Your Worship."

The Chairman said: "Very well, Officer, write it down and hand it up."

He did so. The Chairman read the offending words and passed them to her immediate colleague on her right. He, unfortunately, had just "dropped off" for a moment. She therefore nudged him in the ribs.

He woke up, saw the piece of paper, read the words on it, and said with surprise:

"What, now?"

Sir Frank Hartley, C.B.E., Ph.D., F.P.S., F.R.S.C.,
Vice-Chancellor, University of London, 1976-78.

Verbal Inflation:

I don't want to make a long speech because the most important principles can be briefly expressed.

The Lord's Prayer has 56 words; the Ten Commandments has 297; the American Declaration of Independence has 300; but an E.E.C. directive on the import of caramel and caramel products requires 26,911 words.

The moral is obvious.

Sir Charles Hartwell, C.M.G.,
H.M. Colonial Service, 1927-60.

There was a young lady of Wantage
Of whom the Town Clerk took advantage
Said the Borough Surveyor
Of course you must pay her
You have altered the line of her frontage.

Eric Hartwell,
Vice-Chairman and Joint Chief Executive, Trust Houses Forte Ltd.

Some years ago I visited a small hostelry on the outskirts of Dublin with some friends, and we entered the lounge which was quite simply but comfortably furnished. In one corner of the room was a small hand-operated service lift with a bell press alongside it bearing the notice "Please ring for service."

I rang the bell and nothing happened.

I rang the bell again and still nothing happened.

I then put my finger on the bell push and kept it there, and I could hear it ringing in the basement.

Suddenly a broad Irish female voice called up the lift shaft:

"Are you there, sir?"

I said: "Yes, I am here."

The voice replied:

"Well, I'll be telling you, the more you will be ringing the more I won't come up."

Lieut.-Colonel Harvey Harvey-Jamieson, O.B.E., T.D., D.L.,
Member of The Queen's Bodyguard for Scotland (Royal Company of Archers).

The scene is set in Edinburgh about the turn of the century when trams were the normal form of transport.

My mother was getting out of a tram in Princes Street and picked up what she thought was her umbrella, but the lady in the seat beside her said:

"Excuse me but that is mine."

My mother apologised and then picked up her own much inferior one which had fallen on the floor and was hidden by her voluminous skirts of those days

On her way home from her morning shopping my mother called at a shop to collect her best umbrella, which had been repaired.

On the journey home she found herself sitting in a tram next to the same lady whom she had met earlier. The latter seeing my mother with two umbrellas lent across and said:

"Ah! I see you have had a successful day."

Macdonald Hastings,
Author, Commentator and Journalist.

A famous fast bowler was introduced to an Arab sheik who boasted that he had one hundred and ninety-eight wives.

The bowler retorted:

"You only need another two, and you are entitled to a new ball."

Sir Geoffrey Haworth, Bt., M.A., F.R.S.A.,
Farmer; Chairman, Hallé Concerts Society.

One Sunday in January in one of the mid-western states of America, there was a terrible blizzard blowing. The parson struggled through deep snow to the village church where he found a congregation of one — a cowboy in the front pew solemnly chewing gum.

"Well, cowboy," he said, "it's a terrible morning and there are only two of us. Shall we call it a day and get back to our firesides."

"Well," said the cowboy, "I dunno, I only know about cattle. If I take a load out and only one comes ah still feed him."

Stung by this rebuke, the parson went through the whole morning service, choosing the longer version wherever possible and throwing in a sermon of thirty-five minutes for good measure.

Feeling rather pleased with himself, he again addressed his congregation:

"Well, cowboy, how did I do? Was that all right?"

There was a pause in the rhythmic chewing.

"Well I dunno, I only know about cattle. If I take a load out to feed them and only one comes, ah don't tip the whole load off."

The Late James Haworth,
Member of Parliament for Walton, Liverpool, 1945-50; President, Transport Salaried Staffs Association, 1953-56; Member, London Midland Railway Board, 1956-67.

One Saturday afternoon I found myself in Carlisle. As my meeting was not until the evening, I went to a local football match. As the game progressed I became interested, and amused, in a spectator not far from me, who had appointed himself as instructor to the centre-forward of the Carlisle team. Every time this player got the ball, this fellow shouted his orders: "Shoot", "Pass to your right wing", "Back heel it", "Dribble it" and so on.

But on one occasion the poor centre-forward received the ball, he was completely surrounded by opponents, a long way from the goal and no member of his own side within reach.

What would be our friend's reaction? For half a second, only, he hesitated, but then, he funnelled his hands round his mouth, and yelled at the top of his voice.

"Use your own judgement."

Sir Claude Hayes, K.C.M.G., M.A., M.Litt.,
Chairman, Crown Agents for Overseas Governments and Administrations, 1968-74.

A civil service mandarin received the minutes of a Cabinet meeting, and in accordance with the instruction on them he initialled them and sent them back to the Cabinet office.

Next day they were returned to him with a note:

"It is observed that you have seen and initialled these minutes. You are not authorised to see this class of document. Kindly delete your initials."

He did so and sent the minutes back to the Cabinet office. Next day they were returned to him with another note:

"It is observed that you have made an alteration on this copy of the Cabinet Minutes. Kindly initial it."

Vice-Admiral Sir John Hayes, K.C.B., O.B.E.,
Flag Officer Flotillas, Home Fleet, 1964-66; Flag Officer Scotland and Northern Ireland, 1966-68; Lord Lieutenant of Ross and Cromarty.

In H.M. Ships boats hoisted at davits on the starboard side are given odd numbers — 1st motor boat, 3rd motor boat, etc. — and those at the port davits even numbers. A very small midshipman was (as Damon Runyan would have put it) making no kind of a fist at getting his boat alongside at a port in the South of France during landings in the 1939-45 war. He was watched from above by an American G.I. leaning over the rail.

After watching the midshipman ram the steps twice, the G.I. slowly took the cigarette out of his mouth and drawled:

"Say, Ensign, what d'you call that gasoline gig o' your's down there?"

Stung, the midshipman drew himself up to his full 5ft. 4in. and said rather pompously:

"It's the first motor boat."

"I'll say it is!"

Barney Hayhoe, M.P.,
Minister of State, Civil Service Department.

During the last World War when Queen Wilhelmina's country feared German invasion she is reputed to have sent a telegram to Winston Churchill saying:

"Country in grave peril: will flood dykes before allowing invasion by Germans."

Winston Churchill replied:

"Hold your water till jerries arrive."

Signed: "W.C."

Sir William Hayter, K.C.M.G.,
H.M. Ambassador to U.S.S.R., 1953-57; Warden of New College, Oxford, 1958-76.

I was Ambassador in Moscow in the autumn of 1956, at the time of Suez, when the Soviet authorities mounted a "spontaneous" demonstration against the British Embassy. The demonstrators had been issued with appropriate slogans and brought to the Embassy in factory transport. They were swarming all over the outside of the building and climbing up the walls.

I was told there was a general of the militia (i.e. the civil police) in the crowd outside, and sent someone out to bring him in. He was a very stupid looking man in a fur hat. I was feeling quite cross by then, and said to him in an irritated voice:

"How much longer is this disgraceful scene going on?"

He looked at his wrist-watch and replied:

"About another quarter of an hour."

(I have found that this is a very useful way to bring an after-dinner speech to an end.)

The Rt. Hon. Denis Healey, C.H., M.B.E., M.P.,
Deputy Leader of the Labour Party.

One of my predecessors, as Chancellor of the Exchequer, found it difficult to compose his own after-dinner speeches and therefore delegated the task to his private secretary.

After some years, the worm turned, and when the Chancellor was making his annual speech at the Mansion House, he read it as follows:

"My Lords, Your Grace, My Lord Bishop, My Lords Sheriffs, Ladies and Gentlemen.

"The problem which faces us today is perhaps the most daunting which has ever faced our nation in its island history. Unless we can find a solution in the coming months I see nothing but catastrophe ahead. There are only three possible ways of escape from the dangers now confronting us . . . . . ."

(Then he turned over the page and read out . . . . . .)

"From now on, you're on your own, you bastard!"

Air Marshal Sir Maurice Heath, K.B.E., C.B., C.V.O., D.L.,
Served with the Royal Air Force, 1927-65; Chief Honorary Steward, Westminster Abbey, 1965-74; Extra Gentleman Usher to the Queen.

After the Investiture of Knights Grand Cross of the Order of the British Empire at St. Paul's Cathedral a few years ago a certain Air Chief Marshal was attending the civic luncheon given afterwards by the Lord Mayor of London and found himself seated next to the Lady Mayoress, a good looking and amply proportioned lady who, in addition to her Mayoral chain, carried a red rose in her bosom.

The Air Chief Marshal, who was himself still in his robes and wearing the gold collar, or chain, of the Order, eyed the lady's rose speculatively, and as he sat down next to her said, with a twinkle in his eye:

"Madam, if I were to pluck your rose, would you blush?"

"Air Marshal," replied the Lady Mayoress, without hesitation, "if I were to pull your chain, would you flush?"

Brigadier Simon Heathcote, C.B.E.,
Chief of Staff, Middle East Command, 1962-64.

The beautiful countess returned from the ball and rang for her footman. When he came into her bedroom, she said:

"Edward, take off my shoes," and he did.

Then she said: "Edward, take off my coat," and he did.

Next she asked him to take off her dress and then said:

"And now, Edward, take off all my remaining clothes."

When he had done this, the countess said:

"And now, Edward, if you are to remain in my service, you are never to wear my clothes again."

Sir John Hedges, C.B.E.,
Solicitor; Chairman, Berkshire Area Health Authority, 1973-79.

Coroner to Witness: "The collision occurred at the junction of High Street and Church Road; how far away were you?"

Witness: "54 yards, 2 feet, 6 inches."

Coroner: "You are very precise. Did you measure it?"

Witness: "Yes."

Coroner: "Why?"

Witness: "I knew some idiot would ask me."

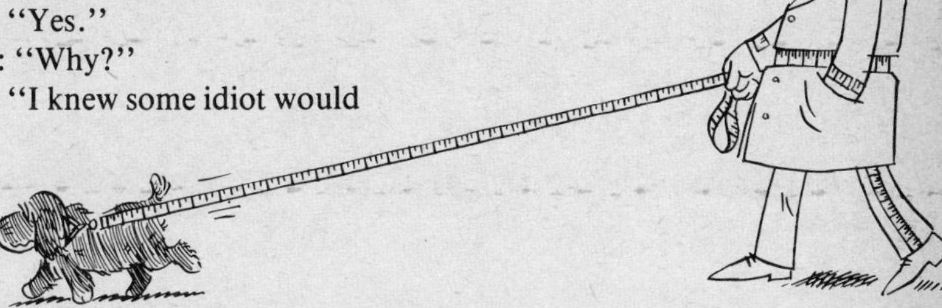

**Sir James Henderson, K.B.E., C.M.G.,
H.M. Ambassador to Bolivia, 1956-60.**

A man was out for a walk in one of our larger cities and he met a penguin, which seemed to take a liking to him, as it followed him. Not knowing what to do with it, he took it to the nearest police station and sought advice.

"Take it to the Zoo," they said.

Next day one of the policemen met the man in the street, still accompanied by the penguin.

"What are you doing, still going round with that creature?" he said. "I thought you were going to take it to the Zoo."

"Oh yes," replied the man, "but that was yesterday. Today we are going to the pictures."

A tourist, driving a car, arrived in this country, and, seeing the yellow line by the side of the road, asked a pedestrian (who happened to be Irish) what it meant.

"Ah, well," he replied, "that means no parking at all."

"Thank you," said the motorist, "but what do two yellow lines mean, then?"

The pedestrian was nonplussed for a moment, but only for a moment.

"Well you see," he said, "that means no parking at all, at all."

**Air Chief Marshal Sir Anthony Heward, K.C.B., O.B.E., D.F.C., A.F.C.,
Air Member for Supply and Organisation, Ministry of Defence, 1973-76.**

Mark Twain was once invited, as the guest of honour, to a dinner at which all the great leaders of the American Civil War were present. When it came to the speeches the military leaders made their rather lengthy and somewhat heavy remarks. In due course Mark Twain was called on to speak and he rose — a shade unsteadily — to his feet.

"Gentlemen," he said, "Caesar is dead; Hannibal is no longer with us; Napoleon has long since passed away; and Wellington is under the sod.

"And — to tell you the truth — I am not feeling too good myself."

And with that he sat down.

Derek Heys, C.B.E., T.D.,
Consul for Belgium in Liverpool, 1966-77.

Mother reading letter from greatly adored young son serving with H.M. Navy as a member of a submarine crew in 1940.

"Dear Mother,

"I am happy to say that I am fit and well and full of life, but unfortunately as you know, I am unable to tell you where I am but you will be interested to know that I shot a polar bear yesterday."

Several weeks later, same mother reading another letter from same son.

"Dear Mother,

"I am happy to say that I am fit and well and thoroughly enjoying myself, but unfortunately as you know, I am unable to tell you where I am but you may be interested to know that last evening I danced with a hula-hula girl."

Same mother reading another letter from same son after a lapse of only two weeks.

"Dear Mother,

"This time I am able to divulge to you that I am in hospital and the doctor tells me that it would have been better had I danced with the polar bear and shot the hula-hula girl."

Sir William Hildred, C.B., O.B.E.,
Director-General, International Air Transport Association, 1946-66.

Wife, listening to her husband on the telephone, hears him say indignantly:

"Don't ask me; ask the Coast Guard; ask the Meteorological Office." When he put the 'phone down she asks:

"Who was that, dear?"
"Some silly ass wanting to know if the coast was clear."

**Sir Austin Bradford Hill, C.B.E., F.R.S., Ph.D., D.Sc.,
Emeritus Professor of Medical Statistics, London School of Hygiene and Tropical Medicine, University of London.**

The notice posted in the Town Hall read:
"During the present fuel crisis officials are advised to take advantage of their typists between the hours of 12 and 2."

The newspaper correspondent cabled to his editor:
"Almost impossible to exaggerate the gravity of the situation here, but I shall do my best."

**Admiral of the Fleet, Lord Hill-Norton, G.C.B.,
Chief of the Defence Staff, 1971-73; Chairman, Military Committee of N.A.T.O., 1974-77.**

A newly commissioned sub-lieutenant was having a drink in the Wardroom one evening when one of his friends came in and complimented him on the cut and style and fit of his uniform. The sub-lieutenant, with a rather self-satisfied smirk, pointed out that he had only just got it from a well-known firm of naval tailors and that it had cost him £150, which accounted for the high quality.
Just as he was about to leave the Mess, the other chap said to him:
"I don't know whether you have noticed it or not, but there is one slight flaw — your left trouser leg is longer than your right."
The Sub was furious and stormed into the tailors next morning to be persuaded that to alter the uniform would ruin the style and cut, and that as there was only about an inch in it why not put his left foot on the bar rail when he was next having a drink in the Wardroom and hoist up the trouser leg.
The next evening another officer came up to compliment him on one of the smartest uniforms he had seen. The Sub recounted how much it had cost and how pleased he was with it, when the other chap pointed out that the left sleeve was longer than the right.

A quick comparison showed that it was, so next morning he again went back to the tailors to complain. Again he was told that to mess about with minor alterations would ruin the cut and the style, and spoil the suit, and as it had again happened at the bar, why not hold his drink in his left hand, put his elbows on the bar and draw his sleeve down below his cuff.

That evening he was again in the Wardroom with his foot perched on the bar rail, trouser hoisted up, a glass held carefully in his left hand and his sleeve pulled down, when the Commander came in and complimented him on his uniform and said how well turned out he was. The Sub again boasted about the £150, when the Commander said he hardly liked to mention it but there was a small ruff on the collar of the jacket, which was standing up about an inch above his shirt collar.

The Sub returned to the tailors once more in a terrible rage but was told that a ruff was not uncommon in a new uniform and that, provided he could keep his head slightly lowered for the next few weeks, the collar of the jacket would settle down.

That evening, when having his drink, with his left foot lodged on the bar rail and trouser hoisted, his left hand at an awkward angle over the bar and his head bent forward, he was approached by a midshipman. The midshipman, having complimented him on the cut and style of his uniform, said how much he wished he had gone to the same tailor for his own, but after they had been talking for a little while he said:

"I hope it won't embarrass you being asked this, but how did a chap like you with one short leg, a deformed left arm and a hump on your back get into the Navy, when I had terrible problems just because one of my feet is a bit flat?"

The Late Joseph Hislop, F.G.S.M.,
Professor of Singing, Guildhall School of Music and Drama, 1952-64.

The late Sir Harry Lauder and I were great friends and whenever possible we came to listen to each other's performances.

It so happened that I was giving a celebrity concert at the Town Hall in Stirling in the year 1924. I had as an assisting artist an excellent pianist — Walter Rummel. He was a very big man — about 6 ft. 3 in. in height, and very powerfully built.

After the concert, Sir Harry and Lady Lauder came round to see me and I introduced them to Rummel. You must bear in mind that Harry Lauder was only about 5 ft. 5 in. in height. After the usual compliments had been exchanged, Harry Lauder turned to Rummel and said:

"I was charmed with your playing, Mr. Rummel, and watched with admiration your fingers moving with great rapidity over the keyboard and I was astonished at the power you got from the instrument, and, Mr. Rummel, I would like to ask you a question. How does it come about that a big strong man like you should be playing the piano instead of working?"

Sir Frederick Hoare, Bt.,
Banker; Lord Mayor of London, 1961-62.

A young curate was very nervous about giving his first sermon and so the vicar suggested that he should try a little whisky beforehand, but warned the curate not to overdo it. However the curate was so anxious to be in good form that he took plenty.

Feeling right on top of his form he asked the vicar afterwards how the sermon had gone.

"Well," said the vicar, "you did simply splendidly. There were, however, one or two little points that weren't quite right. First there were twelve Apostles, not ten, and there were ten Commandments, not twelve. Finally, David did not slay Goliath with a ruddy great axe!"

Sir Julian Hodge, Kt.St.J., K.S.G., LL.D.,
Merchant Banker.

On the occasion when I made my last speech, a young lady came up to me and said:

"I enjoyed your speech sumptuously."

"Thank you very much."

She went on:

"You ought to have your speeches published."

In as self-deprecating a manner as possible, I said:

"Well, perhaps I will have them published posthumously."

"Oh yes, I should," she answered, "and the sooner the better."

Brian Harry Holbeche, C.B.E., M.A.,
Headmaster, King Edward's School, Bath; President, Headmasters' Association, 1970.

The speaker tells how he returns to his school for an Old Boys' Reunion and embellishes this with some nostalgic memories. Because he was head prefect when the war broke out, he finds himself sitting next to the headmaster at dinner. After an excellent dinner at which the wine flows freely, the latter, somewhat advanced in liquor, leans over confidentially to the speaker and enquires:

"Let me see, Smith, was it you or your brother who was killed in the last war?"

Lord Home of the Hirsel, K.T., P.C., D.L.,
The Prime Minister, 1963-64.

A man asks his friend:

"How's your wife?"

To receive the answer:

"Compared to what?"

**Admiral Sir Frank Hopkins, K.C.B., D.S.O., D.S.C.,
Commander-in-Chief Portsmouth, 1966-67.**

The dinner was attended mainly by public relations and advertising people.

In order to stress the importance of their profession I quoted a short rhyme as follows:

The Codfish lays ten thousand eggs
The humble hen lays one
But the Codfish does not cackle
To tell you what she's done
And so we scorn the Codfish
While the humble hen we prize
Which indicates to you and me
It pays to advertise.

**Lord Horder,
Publisher, Composer and Author.**

A small boy and girl were standing in front of a painting of Adam and Eve in the Garden of Eden.

"Which is Adam and which is Eve?" the girl asked the boy.

"Well, I don't rightly know," the boy replied, "but I think I could tell, if they had their clothes on."

**Michael Hordern, C.B.E.,
Actor: Stage, Films, Radio and Television.**

Two actors playing scene in long-running (too long-running) play. Actors have long since forgotten what play is about. One is thinking:

"Why didn't I make that grand slam in hearts between the shows this afternoon?"

The other:

"Where shall I take my girl friend to supper after the show?"

They dry up.

Prompter blows dust off script and whispers a prompt.

No response.
Prompter gives line a bit louder.
No response.
Third time prompter shouts the prompt.
One of the two actors gets wearily to his feet, crosses to the prompt corner and says to the prompter:
"Yes, darling, we heard you the first time but which of us says it?"

**Alistair Allan Horne, M.A., F.R.S.L.,
Author, Journalist, Farmer and Lecturer.**

Four peppery French generals had a habit of playing bridge together every evening in the Mess.
One night, the fourth was taken ill and a young lieutenant was asked to fill his place. In terror at playing in such exalted company, the young lieutenant went on from one appalling blunder to another. Finally he said to his enraged partner:
"Je regrette, mon Général, mais je pense que je dois me retirer."
The general growled, without so much as looking up:
"Plutôt ton père!"

Colonel Sir Andrew Horsbrugh-Porter, Bt., D.S.O.

About eight miles from where I was born there is a crossroad between Bargycastle and Tom Haggard; on one side of the road, more or less embedded in the bank is a large white stone.
On certain nights of the year a ghostly figure is reputed to be seen sitting on this stone, casting a baleful eye on any midnight traveller. Needless to say even the boldest prefer to have a companion when going past the crossroad at a late hour.
Michael Kehoe, however, was no believer in the supernatural and "dismissed" the story as a bit of "codology". He and his friend, Tom Prendergast, were having an argument at a mutual friend's house, Tom being a firm believer in the truth of the story.
It was settled that both would pass the crossroad on their way home.
When it was near midnight, the bold Michael slipped out of the house, ran down to the crossroad and seated himself on the stone. Presently he heard

Tom coming along the road. The moon in its last quarter cast a ghostly half-light with deep shadows over the crossroad. Michael sat still and saw Tom give a horrified glance at him and hurry off home.

Next morning he sought out Tom, prepared to pull his leg and finally lay the ghost.

"Well Tom," says he, "I suppose you saw the ghost on the stone last night?"

"I did so," said Tom.

"Well now," says Michael, "it was no ghost at all only meself that was sitting on it — so there's your old yarn for you."

"Yes," replied Tom, "I could see *you* plain enough in the moonlight, *but you were not the only one there."*

Major-General Derek Horsford, C.B.E., D.S.O.

At a private dinner party, during the main course, the dog of the house kept jumping up the male guest sitting on our hostess's left. The dog would put his paws on the man's leg and try and lick him and kept wagging his tail.

With a smug smile the man said to the assembled company:

"You know, it's a funny thing but dogs always love me."

To which our hostess replied:

"I wouldn't be too sure about that. We are rather short of crockery and you are eating off his plate."

Jack Howarth,
Stage and Television Actor.

3 a.m. Paddy is awakened by the 'phone ringing. He gets out of bed and goes downstairs — picks up the 'phone saying:

"Hello."

"Hello. Is that Belfast double two, double two?"

"No," says Paddy. "This is Belfast two two, two two."

"Ho. I am sorry that you've been troubled."

"It's all right," Paddy replied. "I had to come down as the 'phone was ringing."

Lord Howick of Glendale,
Merchant Banker; Member of Executive Committee, National Art Collections Fund.

The most precarious profession I have come across involved a man who made his living by hitting crocodiles on the head with a stick with a lump of lead stuck on the end, to knock them out. He lived by a lake in Africa and used to wade out up to waist height at night with a miner's lamp on his head, looking around until the light caught the reflection of a pair of eyes; he would then fasten the light on to the eyes to dazzle them and slowly approach to within three or four feet, at which point the crocodile would make a lunge at him. Stepping smartly to one side, he would hit it as hard as he could just behind one of the eyes with his stick, to knock it out, tie a rope around one leg and tow it off to the shore in order to shoot it with a revolver very carefully, so as not to damage the valuable part of the skin.

There were two hazards to contend with.

The first was when the crocodile woke up on the way to the shore, in which case he was hanging on to a rope with a crocodile with a sore head at the other end; the only thing to do then was to let go of the rope and hope.

The second hazard was that there was no way of telling the difference at night between the eyes of a crocodile and the eyes of a hippopotamus, and it's no use hitting a hippo over the head with anything; they also have a habit of biting people in half and the only clue he got that he was approaching a hippo was when the eyes disappeared under water when he was about four yards away. Hippos don't swim, they bounce along the bottom, which was why he did not like going deeper than waist high since he liked to feel that he could run faster through a lake than a bouncing hippo, and he did not like the idea of being bitten in half.

Unfortunately, one day, or rather night, he was.

The moral may be that if you must live dangerously, do so for something more worthwhile than ladies' handbags.

Lord Cledwyn of Penrhos, C.H., P.C.,
Chairman of the Parliamentary Labour Party, 1974-79; former Secretary of State for Wales and Minister of Agriculture.

We must always be careful to question the belief, which is current in some quarters, that Governments and great Departments of State know what is best for people.

Some years ago, an Anglesey man from the famous village of Llanerchymedd visited London for the first time. On his first day, he was caught in the rush hour in Piccadilly tube station. The confusion was a new experience and he found himself bundled here and there and he lost his hat.

Somehow, he found his way to the street and to a big hat shop. In response to his enquiry, a shop assistant brought four or five new hats for his inspection. After trying them on, he chose one and asked how much it was. On being told that it was five pounds, he said:

"Good Heavens! I could get one exactly like that in Llanerchymedd for thirty shillings."

"That may well be so," replied the assistant, "but you see, we have very large windows here full of hats and sometimes they get faded. We then send them to places like Llanerchymedd, where they are sold cheap."

The Welshmen completed the purchase reluctantly, but he had to have his hat, and as he was leaving, the assistant said:

"It is a coincidence, but my wife happens to come from Llanerchymedd. She was Ellen Jones and she lived in the Mill. You may have known her?"

"Know her!" he replied, "I knew her well. She was a pretty girl. You won't mind me saying that I took her out for a walk many times."

He paused and then said:

"But when things get a little faded in Llanerchymedd, we send them to London."

Field Marshal Sir Richard Hull, K.G., G.C.B., D.S.O., D.L.,
Chief of the Defence Staff, 1965-67; Constable of H.M. Tower of London, 1970-75.

A very successful young tycoon lost his business flair and was so worried he went to his doctor for a medical check up.

His G.P. could find nothing medically wrong with him and suggested that he should see a brain specialist.

This he did, and was told that his brain was prematurely old and worn out but not to worry as with modern brain transplant surgery he could be given a new one.

He asked about the cost, and the reply was that it all depended on what type of brain he wanted — for instance, he could have a legal brain for £5,000, or a good medical brain for £10,000 or an Army officer's brain for £25,000.

"That's preposterous! An officer's brain can't cost more than twice as much as a doctor's!"

"Oh, yes," was the reply. "You see, it's as good as new; it has never been used."

Christmas Humphreys, Q.C.,
A Permanent Judge of the Central Criminal Court, 1968-76.

Two men would habitually meet in a pub, but suddenly one of them ceased to come. Months later he reappeared and his friend asked him where he'd been.

"Inside," said Bill.

"Gorblimey, what for?"

"Nothing," said Bill. "It was like this. On my way to work I pass the local police station, and one day a copper put his head out of the gate and asked me to come in. 'What for?' I asked, suspicious like, though I had a good record. 'To help us,' he said, 'on an identification parade. You just stand in a line and a witness picks out the bloke who done it. It don't take long and you get a cup of tea after'.

"So I went in, curious like, and a lot just like me sort of stood in a line in the yard. Then a door opened, and the most gorgeous, curvy volupshus young blonde I've ever seen came straight towards us. The bloke in charge said something and she walked down the line. When she came to me, she said, all excited, 'That's him'. 'Touch him on the shoulder', said the bloke in charge. She did and I felt hot and oozy-like inside."

"Well," said his friend, as Bill seemed wrapped up in his memory, "What happened then?"

"Well," said Bill, "the rest just oozed away and I was taken into the station and a sergeant told me I was under arrest and he was going to charge me. I was still looking at the blue-eyed bundle of she'd-got-it, but the sergeant made me listen to his list."

"Well?" said the friend as Bill again fell silent.

"I l-listened," said Bill, nearly upsetting his beer with emotion at the memory, "and when I heard w-what I had d-done to that g-girl I was so p-proud that I p-pleaded g-guilty."

A famous man's club decided to allow women members. A distinguished Q.C. was instructed to apply in a Chancery Court for the necessary permission to alter the wording in the founding document of the club. A pile of documents was produced by the Q.C.'s clerk and placed before him, and another set before his junior behind him; and another before the solicitor in front.

His Lordship prepared to listen patiently.

The Q.C. made ponderous remarks on the passage of time, the changing fashions of society, and hinted at pecuniary advantage which might arise from the proposed change. He then laboriously pointed out page after page the necessary alterations in the document, adding "or she" to "he" and the like, and finally sat down.

His Lordship graciously approved all alterations, and the Q.C. and the junior and the solicitor and their clerks who gathered up the documents, rose to depart, when a voice from the Bench re-called them.

"Sir Hezekiah."

"My Lord?"

"Before you leave the Court it occurs to me that one of the phrases in the document still before me might be worthy of your attention."

The Q.C., his junior, the solicitor and their clerks all returned to their seats.

His Lordship: "Would you be so good as to glance at the opening sentence of the object of the club, Sir Hezekiah?"

Sir Hezekiah glanced, the junior glanced, the solicitor glanced, and all with difficulty stifled an embarrassed guffaw.

The first object of the club, unaltered, ran:

"The object of the club is to encourage intercourse between the members."

Sir Olliver Humphreys, C.B.E., B.Sc., F.Inst.P., F.I.E.E., F.R.Ae.S., Founder Chairman, Conference of the Electronics Industry, 1963-67.

In the days when electricity supplies were being converted from direct to alternating current a friend of mine returned from holiday to find a trench dug along the full length of the road outside his house in Harrow-on-the-Hill.

Being of an enquiring disposition he went, after dinner, to see a friend of his who was a classics master in the School and asked him what was happening.

"I am not quite sure," his friend replied, "but I understand that it is something to do with the electricity — I believe that they are changing us from B.C. to A.D."

John Leonard Hunt, M.P., U.K. Representative at the Council of Europe and Western European Union, 1973-77.

A rather pompous politician decided to go on an early-morning tour of the docks in his constituency. It was a bitterly cold morning and, after walking around the wharves for half an hour, the Member of Parliament was "taken short". He went up to a docker standing by the quayside.

"Excuse me my man," he said, "can you tell me where the urinal is?"

The docker looked him up and down and then replied:

"'Aven't gotta clue mate — how many funnels has it got?"

Dr. Robert Hurst, C.B.E., G.M., Director of Research, British Ship Research Association, 1963-76.

An Irishman was gloating to his friend as he came through the ticket barrier:

"I've done British Rail at last — I've got a return ticket and I'm not going back!"

Sir Peter Hutchison, Bt.,
Clerk of the Peace and County Solicitor, East Suffolk, 1970-72.

A Cambridge professor used to speak so slowly that undergraduates who attended his lectures became bored and impatient and his audiences diminished. At last one of his pupils summoned up courage to tell him candidly, why the lectures were so poorly attended.

"I know . . . I speak . . . so slowly," said the professor, "but my sister . . . she speaks . . . much more slowly . . . than I do. She went out one day . . . and she was accosted . . . by a man. . . . She said to him . . . 'I am not that sort of girl . . . at all.' . . . But she spoke too slowly . . . and before . . . she had finished speaking . . . she *was*!"

Sir Noël Hutton, G.C.B., Q.C.,
First Parliamentary Counsel, 1956-68.

My brother, Charles Hutton, had been attending a C.C.C. dinner at which Edward Pearce (then a puisne judge, now Lord Pearce), gave them the original Latin version of "pin-up" — *virgo tintacta.*

The Rev. John Huxtable, D.D.,
Executive Officer, Churches Unity Commission, 1975-78.

Grandpa and grandma had arrived to visit the family; and since the house was modest in size the best bedroom was given over to them.

Their small grandson, aged about 2½ years, was used to going into this bedroom each morning to get into bed with his parents.

On the first morning of this visit he found that grandparents are not as open to this custom as parents.

On the second day of the visit, the grandson pushed his luck again, only to find that Grandpa had already gone to the bathroom to shave. Grandma was already out of bed. She had taken off her nightie and had nothing on at all, as she looked for whatever she put on first.

The grandson looked at her with great interest and exclaimed:

"Grandma! You do look funny without your glasses!"

Rutherford Graham Ikin, M.A.,
Headmaster of Trent College, 1936-68.

A young man — nervous at the thought of making an after-dinner speech — was told by a clergyman not to worry. He said that he could preach a sermon on any subject at a moment's notice.

To prove this, on the following Sunday, a slip of paper was handed to him as he went into the pulpit on which was written one word — "constipation".

Without any demur he said:

"My text is taken from the Book of Exodus, Chapter 34.

"And Moses took the tablets and went up into the mountain."

I am not like that clergyman. I am very nervous.

Sir John Inch, C.V.O., C.B.E., Q.P.M.,
Chief Constable, Edinburgh City Police, 1955-75.

Gamekeeper Tamas had a family of nine. He was very friendly with the local doctor and they often shot together.

Tamas's wife was very ill at the birth of the ninth child and the doctor told Tamas that it had been touch and go as to whether the mother or child had to be sacrificed. In the end they were both well but the doctor told Tamas that his wife should have no more children. This was on the last day of the shooting and the doctor added:

"In sporting parlance, Tamas, put away your gun."

At the beginning of the next shooting season, the doctor and Tamas met. The doctor told Tamas that he was very angry with him, because despite his emphatic words, Tamas's wife was again expecting.

Tamas replied that the blame was not all his. He had reported the doctor's conversation about laying by his gun to his wife and she had replied:

"Well if you do that, Tamas, I'll let the shooting."

**The Late Lord Inman, P.C., J.P.,
President of Charing Cross Hospital;
Liveryman of London; Author;
Former Cabinet Minister and
Chairman of the B.B.C.**

A rather simple soul had been persuaded to go to the harvest festival service at the village church. He was seated in the front pew and just in front of him was a delightful assortment of fruit. His eye fell on a dish of delicious plums and, thinking they were for the congregation, he soon finished the lot.

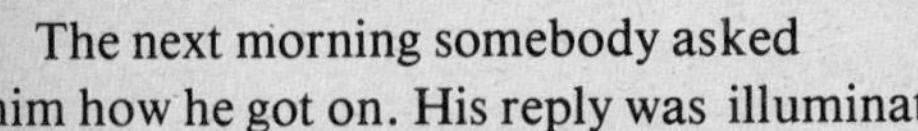

The next morning somebody asked him how he got on. His reply was illuminating.

"Oh, they were very kind to me. They put a dish of plums in front of me and soon afterwards they came round with a plate for the stones."

A visiting clergyman went to a small village to take the evening service as the resident parson was ill. As he had not been there before, he arrived in good time and had a look round the church. He saw a collecting box with a card over it "For church expenses", and into it he put 20p.

When the service was over, the verger came into the vestry with the collecting box. He said:

"It has always been our custom to give the contents of this box to any visiting clergyman we may have."

He selected a key from a bunch he held and, after opening it, he said:

"My word, sir, you are lucky tonight, there's 20p in it," and he handed the money over.

When he reached home, the clergyman told his wife and small daughter of his experience. The girl's answer was:

"Well, you see, daddy, if you had put more into the box, you would have got more out of it."

Fergus Munro Innes, C.I.E., C.B.E.,
Chairman, India General Navigation and Railway Company, 1973-78.

The speaker was talking about the tension of golf. An important foursome match went to the last green. One man was left with a 10ft putt to halve the match. He studied the line from the back of the hole, he studied it from the front. He lined up to putt. There was a long pause. You could see he was in an agony of concentration and tension. Just as he was making his stroke a small dog ran between the ball and the hole. The putt went in.

His partner ran over delightedly saying:

"Partner, I don't know how you did it, with that dog running across and all."

"Good heavens," the man replied. "You don't mean to say that was a *real* dog!"

The Late Air Chief Marshal Sir Ronald Ivelaw-Chapman, G.C.B., K.B.E., D.F.C., A.F.C.,
Vice-Chief of the Air Staff, 1953-57 (Prisoner of War, 1944-45).

In 1953 there was a London to Wellington (New Zealand) air race in which the Royal Air Force was competing with a team of Canberra aircraft. I was at the time Vice-Chief of the Air Staff and Air Chief Marshal Sir Donald Hardman was Chief of the Air Staff of the Royal Australian Air Force.

It so happened that Donald Hardman and I arrived in the same car at the Wellington destination airfield at about 1 a.m. and some hour or so before the first contestant was expected. Rain was deluging from the sky and we were met by an absolute shambles — a seething mass of cars and pedestrians surging forward in opposite directions and blinding spot-lights everywhere.

The driver of our service car had been told to take us to the V.I.P. reception hangar where all the ceremonial of the first arrival was due to take place. But he was flummoxed as much as we were and could get no coherent answers to his repeated questioning as to where he should take us.

Then, suddenly, a pedestrian in a reach-me-down mackintosh (who may have seen our uniforms in the light of a spot-light) stepped forward from the crowd and said:

"I expect you gentlemen are looking for the reception hangar. Straight ahead and second turn on the right. I don't expect you know me, but my name is Holland and I happen to be the Prime Minister."

That was true humility if you like!

Michael Ivens,
Director, Aims for Freedom and Enterprise; Author and Poet.

A young man found himself sitting next to an incredibly attractive and interesting woman at a dinner party. During the course of the meal he felt her leg pressing against his. As the dinner continued, he experienced extraordinary feelings of elation, significance and an enormous sense of communication with her. It was clearly one of the ecstatic moments of his life.

And, as the dinner ended, he suddenly became aware that his leg was pressed — not against the lady's — but against the table leg.

Stephen Jack, F.R.S.A.,
Actor.

There are innumerable stories (many apocryphal) attributed to Dr. Spooner. The following story, I was assured by the friend who passed it on to me many years ago, is authentic.

Spooner was walking down the High one day when he met a young student of his acquaintance, to whom he said:

"Ah, dear man, delighted to see you. Do come to breakfast on Wednesday — I've got Thompson coming."

The young man looked mystified and a little embarrassed. He said:

"It's very kind of you, sir . . . but I *am* Thompson."

To which Spooner replied:

"Oh dear, how very stupid of me — of *course* . . . but do come all the same — I think you'll like him."

An elephant, crashing through the jungle, noticed a movement near one of his fore-hooves. He stopped and peered down. A tiny creature peeped up at him. The elephant said:

"What are *you*?"

A tiny voice replied: "I'm a mouse."

Elephant: "You're very *small*."

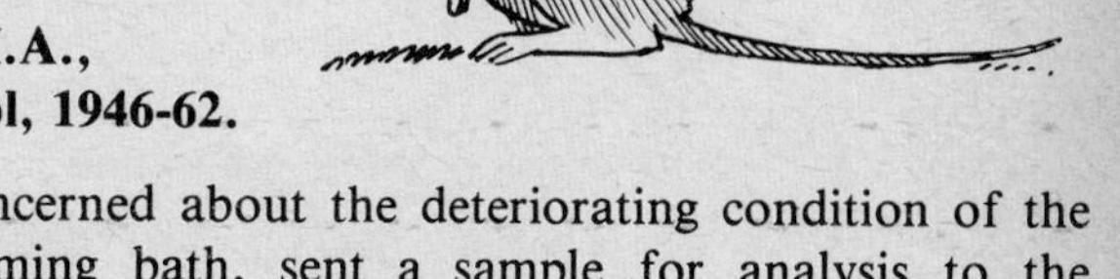

Mouse: "I know — but I haven't been very well."

Hector Beaumont Jacks, M.A.,
Headmaster, Bedales School, 1946-62.

A headmaster, much concerned about the deteriorating condition of the water in his school swimming bath, sent a sample for analysis to the appropriate authority. The report that came back was:

"This horse is past work and should be destroyed."

Francis Jackson,
Organist and Master of the Music, York Minster.

Two cows are looking over the hedge at the passing traffic and they see among it a large tanker proclaiming in large letters on its side:

"Try our tuberculin tested milk — pasteurised — sterilised — homogenised"

Buttercup turns ruefully to her neighbour and says:

"I say, Claribel, it makes you feel kind of inadequate, doesn't it."

Sir Geoffrey Jackson, K.C.M.G.,
H.M. Ambassador to Uruguay, 1969-72.

Going down the street when I was working in Central America I saw the horizontal form of a customer propelled out of the waist-high Western-style swing-doors of a saloon. He picked himself up, staggered to his mule, and tried to clamber aboard and homeward, mumbling as he hauled in vain:

"San Pedro, help me!"

Having slithered down, he wobbled back a couple of paces, saying:

"San Pedro and San Paulo, help me!"

He still finished up on his knees in the dust, so this time he staggered well back, and launched himself yet again, bellowing now:

"San Pedro, San Paulo, and all the saints — help me on my mule!"

It was to such effect that he shot right across the saddle, head-first, and landed nose-down on the other side. He sat up, saw us all laughing, scratched his head and grinned, and commented ruefully:

"Well — I didn't ask them all to help me at once!"

Tom Jackson,
General Secretary, Union of Post Office Workers.

Two Russian workers, Ivan and Boris, were discussing the possibility of going to work at a construction site in Siberia. They had been told that conditions at the site were excellent and that wages were good. However, rather than both of them taking the risk of finding matters less than good, it was agreed that one would go and write to the other.

Ivan lost the toss of the coin and agreed to go. They then discussed the difficulty of the letter which would be sent describing conditions. Ivan said he was not anxious to send a letter saying that conditions were bad and it was agreed that if the letter were written in blue ink it would be true. On the other hand, if it were in red ink it needed to be taken with a large pinch of salt.

Some weeks passed and the letter arrived. Boris observed it was in blue ink and read it with interest.

"Dear Boris,

"The conditions here are very good, safety, health and welfare provided for. The living accommodation is excellent. The supermarket has everything. Fresh bread daily, sausages, pork and every kind of meat. Clothing can be bought cheaply. In fact I can buy many more things here than in Moscow. There seems to be only one shortage. Unfortunately I cannot buy red ink!!"

Gordon Jacob, C.B.E., D.Mus., F.R.C.M., Hon. R.A.M.,
Composer and Conductor; Professor of Theory, Composition and Orchestration, Royal College of Music, 1924-66.

Candidate on coming out of music examination room:

"I think the examiner must be a very religious man, he keeps putting his head in his hands and saying, 'Oh, my God!'."

Arthur David Jacobs, M.A.,
Head of Music Department, Huddersfield Polytechnic; Editor, British Music Yearbook, 1971-79.

Jewish matron telling another of the tribulations experienced at her holiday hotel:

" . . . . And, my dear, the food there is poison — and such small portions!"

Frederick Jaeger,
Actor.

To a small boy looking urgently for the cloakroom, the huge curved foyer of the Berlin State Opera seemed endless. Earlier he had sat attentively enough between father and mother listening to a gala performance of Mozart's "Magic Flute", and had fidgeted uneasily throughout an interval painfully elongated by a sudden unheralded harangue from a smallish, black-haired man in immaculate evening clothes, flanked by numerous uniformed aides in what had once been the Imperial Box.

His pale face contorted with passion, the familiar lock of hair trembling across his forehead, he had ranted and gestured his diatribe at the enraptured spectators for well over an hour, and even a small boy of eight, dressed in a replica of the "Eton Suit", so fashionable on the Continent in the mid 1930s, would have been frowned upon had he been so bold as to leave his seat until the Führer had completed his message to the citizens of the Third Reich.

Subsequently, the last part of the "Magic Flute" had seemed interminable, and now the need to find the "Gents" was pressing.

Eventually, relief having been obtained, he emerged to find the previously half-empty foyer thronged with departing spectators and, anxious to return to his waiting parents, he began to thread his way through the tail coats and furs pressing towards the exit doors.

Almost at once he became aware of a double line of S.S. guards and brown-shirted storm troopers, who had formed a lane between him and his objective, which stretched from the doors of the inner auditorium to the line of gleaming limousines drawn up by the pillars flanking the main entrance. Already shouts of "Sieg Heil" filled his ears, and in an endeavour to reach his father, whose anxious face he could just discern in the distance, he slipped between the lines of shiny jackboots only to blunder into the black-suited legs of the man from the Imperial Box; looking up he was briefly aware of the white, powdered face, dark burning eyes over a small black moustache, a faint, musky aroma . . .

Never one to lose an opportunity of demonstrating his well-publicised affection for children, the Führer just had time to pat the head of the small blond, blue-eyed boy before burly security guards bustled him away and into the care of his waiting parents.

It was many years before I began to understand why my father, his face white with apprehension, had snatched my hand so roughly and dragged me so unceremoniously into the waiting car. Not a word was spoken on the homeward journey; soon I was packed off to bed, wondering vaguely what I had done wrong by bumping accidentally into a strange man, even if he had seemed to be someone of importance?

Evan Maitland James,
Steward of Christ Church, Oxford, 1963-78.

What's funny about a pair of legs?
The bottom's at the top.

Walter James, M.A.,
Editor, *The Times Educational Supplement*, 1952-69; Principal St. Catharine's, Windsor.

"Horse sense is the kind of extra sense that horses have which leads them not to bet on human beings."

The Hon. Greville Janner, Q.C., M.P.,
Author and Journalist.

The chairman of the company called the managing director into the board room; he was then followed by the next director in seniority; then by another, and all the way down the line until about half an hour later, the most junior and newly appointed director was duly summoned. He found his colleagues sitting around the board room table.

"Sit down, Charles," said the chairman. "Now then. Have you been having an affair with my secretary?"

"Certainly not."

"Are you quite sure?"

"Of course I am. I never laid a finger on her."

"Are you prepared to swear to that?"

"Yes."

"Very well, Charles," said the chairman ominously. "Then *you* sack her!"

Sir Clifford Jarrett, K.B.E., C.B.,
Chairman, Tobacco Research Council, 1971-78.

Among the patients of a certain doctor were a family of mother, father and four children. As he got to know them he was struck by the affection which seemed to unite them all and the happy serenity in which they lived. He was therefore surprised to discover by chance that the parents were not married. Eventually his curiosity got the better of him and he said to the mother:

"I suppose you must have some ideological objection to the state of matrimony, because here you are with a happy, growing family and you are obviously fond of their father and yet you are not married to him."

To which she replied:

"Oh, it's not like that at all. You see, when I was about sixteen I had a spell of heart trouble, which eventually got better and the doctor said I would be all right *provided* I took things gently. I asked him what that meant and, after humming and ha-ing a bit, he said, 'Well, for example, I think you would be unwise to get married'.

"So me and my Fred decided that it would be safer for me if we skipped the wedding ceremony."

Clive Jenkins,
General Secretary, Association of Scientific, Technical and Managerial Staffs.

At a Harvard seminar on the future of profit and industrial relations an American banking president, after listening to me on European movements towards industrial democracy and equity as opposed to the negations and drift in the United States, said:

"Jenkins, it isn't *all* bad here. The buffalo are breeding — and the railroads are becoming extinct."

Hugh Jenkins,
Politician, Broadcaster and Lecturer; Minister for the Arts, 1974-76.

Marlon Brando is said to have defined an actor as:
"A guy who, if you ain't talkin' about him, he ain't listenin'."
To that I would add my own definition of a politician in the same style:
"A politician is a guy, who, if he ain't talking, he ain't listening!"

The Late Leslie Westover Jenkins, C.B.E.,
Chairman, Forestry Commission, 1965-70.

The Scots are famous for keeping the Sabbath and everything else they can lay their hands on.

The Welshmen prey on their knees and their neighbours.

The Irishmen do not know what they want, but are prepared to die for it.

And the Englishmen — are a race of self-made men, thereby relieving the Almighty of a dreadful responsibility.

Winston Churchill once said he was flattered when crowds came to hear him speak, except that:

"On reflection, the crowds would be even greater if they came to see me hanged."

Quote from St. Paul: "Be not forgetful to entertain strangers for thereby have some entertained angels unawares."

Owen Jennings, R.W.S., R.E., A.R.C.A., F.R.S.A.,
Artist; Principal, School of Art, Tunbridge Wells, 1934-65.

A young man having gone to some festivity was introduced to a lady and had the temerity to ask for a dance.

After a rather disastrous start he felt it incumbent upon him to make some kind of explanation, and apology — he said:

"I'm afraid you'll think me awfully clumsy but I'm a little stiff from badminton."

To which she replied:

"I don't care where you come from, but I do wish you'd keep off my feet."

Percival Henry Jennings, C.B.E.,
Director-General, Overseas Audit Service, 1960-63.

The Colonial Secretary, being asked by a lady admirer:
Mr. Secretary, where are the Virgin Islands?''
Replied after some thought:
''Madam, as far away from the Isle of Man as we could put them.''

Sir Maynard Jenour, T.D., J.P.,
Industrialist; Vice Lord Lieutenant of Gwent, 1974-79.

Dai and Blodwen had been married for many years but had no children. Dai went off to work in a local factory while Blodwen stayed at home. One morning she did not feel at all well so went to the doctor. After a thorough examination he said to her:

''Well, Mrs. Davies, I am very pleased to tell you you are pregnant.''

Blodwen was delighted — rushed home — picked up the telephone — rang the factory — eventually got through to Dai's supervisor and said:

''I must speak to Dai at once — most important — very urgent.''

After some demur, the supervisor went up to Dai and said:

''Dai, you're wanted on the telephone.''

Dai picked up the telephone and said ''Ullo''.

Blodwen shouted excitedly down the phone:

''Dai, I'm pregnant.''

Dead silence from Dai till Blodwen could stand it no longer and shouted:

''Dai, I tell you I'm pregnant, can't you say something?''

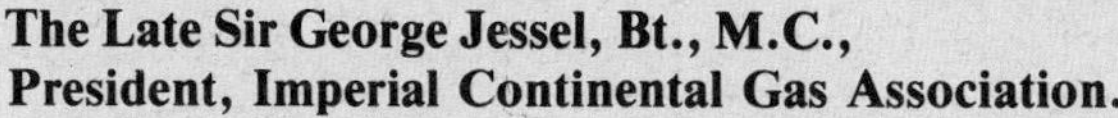

And Dai said:

''Who's speaking?''

The Late Sir George Jessel, Bt., M.C.,
President, Imperial Continental Gas Association.

The Dean of Balliol, A.L. Smith, had several lovely marriageable daughters but often deplored his lack of money.

"But," said a friend, "Your riches are your lovely daughters."

The dean replied:

"But you know one has to husband one's resources."

The Late Sir Richard Jessel,
Member of Advisory Council, Export Credits Guarantee Department, 1950-60.

Mr. Levy had a telephone message from his bank manager telling him that his bank account was overdrawn by £200 and Mr. Levy said to the bank manager:

"What about it?"

"Don't you realise," said the bank manager, "how serious it is to be overdrawn at our bank?"

"Oh," said Mr. Levy, "What was the state of my account this time last week?"

"I will go and look," said the bank manager.

When he came back he said:

"You were £300 in credit."

"Well," said Mr. Levy, "did I ring you up about it?"

David Dilwyn John, C.B.E., T.D., D.Sc., LL.D.,
Director, National Museum of Wales, 1948-68; Holder of the Polar Medal.

This is a true story concerning my gun-site on an Orkney Island in 1943.

The roads and paths were poor and I had set out to improve them with stones, collected in sandbags by the gunners from the surrounding heathland.

In periods of bad weather we were directed by higher authority to "educate" the men. I sought — though inadequately equipped for the purpose — to interest them in their immediate surroundings and once talked about the geological history of our island.

It was, I said, composed of what geologists know as the Old Red Sandstone, laid down in a sea three million years ago; other deposits were superimposed on it; there had been elevation above the surface of the sea; weathering and denudation had taken place, and the Old Red Sandstone was now exposed to our sight.

"So," I concluded, "when next you go to collect stones for the paths, think how old they are."

And I paused — so that they might think. It was a mistake, for a lugubrious gunner in the front row said to me:

"Seems a shame to move 'em, don't it sir?"

Sir Ronald Johnson, C.B., J.P.,
Secretary of Commissions for Scotland, 1972-78.

In a Highland village there was an Armistice Day gathering attended by all the local clergy and other big-wigs, and the laird and his wife offered refreshments afterwards. At the end of the service the bishop made a smart getaway to the Big Hoose and was already sitting in the ingleneuk with a goblet in his hand when the Free Kirk minister arrived.

"Come away, Mr. MacTavish," cries the hostess, "will you take a dram this cold morning?"

The minister raised his hands in horror.

"My dear lady," he said, "I never touch spirits. I would as soon commit adultery as drink a glass of whisky."

The bishop looked up from his corner.

"Your ladyship," he said, "didn't tell me that there was a choice."

There was a travelling circus that owned a gorilla. He was their pride and joy, but he pined for his African forests, and when they set out on a tour of the Highlands, he lay down and died. The circus men did not think it would do to arrive in Inverness with a dead gorilla, so in the Pass of Drumochter, in the middle of the night, they left the poor creature in the ditch.

Early next morning along came two gillies, and stopped short at this foreign apparition.

"Whit like is this, Angus?" said one.

The other took off his bonnet (out of reverence) and scratched his head.

"I'm not rightly knowing, Donald," he said, "yon's no red enough for a MacGregor."

"Aye, Angus, but a Campbell would be blacker."

"Ye're no thinking it's a MacAulay, are ye, it's unco big for that."

So they puzzled each other, until at last Angus said:

"I'll tell you whit way it is, Donald, we'll juist awa' ben the hotel and speir if ony of they English visitors is missing."

(Submitted in memory of the late Sir Duncan Weatherstone, Lord Provost of Edinburgh about 12 years ago, whose favourite story it was.)

Hugh R. Jolly, M.A., M.D., F.R.C.P., D.C.H.,
Physician-in-Charge, Department of Paediatrics, Charing Cross Hospital.

Two African doctors were walking along a river in Africa when they suddenly saw a drowning man. They rushed to help him, brought him to the bank, resuscitated him with mouth to mouth breathing and then organised a mammy wagon to take him the many miles to the nearest hospital for treatment.

They then went back and started their walk again, only to find another drowning man. Having gone through exactly the same procedure, they got back to the river bank only to find yet one more drowning man. After resuscitating him and then another, they found they were doing this all day.

At this point one of the doctors said to the other:

"This is a place we must build a hospital because this is the place where people drown."

The other one then started to walk up-stream, when he heard a shout from his colleague:

"Hey, come quickly, there is another drowning man."

Undeterred, he continued his walk up-stream, saying:

"I'm going to find out who is pushing them in!"

Sir Glyn Jones, G.C.M.G., M.B.E.,
Diplomat; Governor-General of Malawi, 1964-66.

A British businessman visiting an office in Madrid at 3 p.m. one week-day was disconcerted to find no one on duty. He roused the caretaker in the basement and asked:

"Do they not work in the afternoons in Madrid?

"That is not correct," came the answer. "It is in the mornings that they don't work. In the afternoons we have the siesta."

Air Chief Marshal Sir John Whitworth Jones, G.B.E., K.C.B., Member for Supply and Organisation, Air Council, 1952-54.

A distinguished politician, noted for prolixity, was invited with his wife to an official dinner where he was to make a speech. The moment arrived, the toastmaster "prayed silence" for the distinguished statesman, who rose amid respectful hand clapping, began his speech — and went on and on.

Eventually, his wife passed him a little note at which he glanced, brought his speech to a close and sat down.

The wifely aphorism which had silenced him was:

"Albert, a speech does not have to be eternal to be immortal."

Frank Judd,
Director, Voluntary Service Overseas; formerly Minister of State, Foreign and Commonwealth Office.

At a recent N.A.T.O. meeting three admirals were conferring and discussing the nature of courage. They could not agree.

"I vill show you vat is ze nature of courage," expostulated the German admiral, summoning one of his seamen to him.

"You see zat 100 metre flag pole over zere? I vish you to climb to ze top, salute, and jump off!"

The German sailor immediately obeyed, ran to the flag pole, climbed swiftly up, saluted smartly and jumped down.

"Well, that is very impressive," said the American admiral, "but let me now show you what we have come to regard as courage in the history of the United States Navy." Summoning an American sailor, he said:

"You see that 200 metre flag pole? I want you to climb to the top of that flag pole, salute twice and jump off."

At the double the American sailor carried out the command, climbed to the top, saluted and jumped off.

"Well, gentlemen, that was a jolly impressive show," said the British admiral, "but I shall now show you the nature of courage as we understand it in the Royal Navy."

Calling to a rating he told him:

"You see that 300 metre flag pole over there? I want you to climb to the top, salute three times, and jump off."

"What, me, sir?" responded the rating in a tone of incredulity, "You must be bloody daft, sir!"

"There, gentlemen," said the British admiral, "we have the true nature of courage."

Ernest Kay, F.R.G.S.,
Journalist and Publisher.

A rich industrialist from New York City expressed the wish to be buried in Miami in his gold-plated Cadillac.

Came the day.

He was dressed in his white tuxedo suit and laid in the car. An enormous hole was dug in the ground and the Cadillac (with contents) hoisted thirty feet up, ready for the big drop.

"Gee," said one of the onlookers, "that's livin'!"

Alexander James Kellar, C.M.G., O.B.E.,
Attached War Office, 1941-65; English Tourist Board, 1970-73.

A doctor driving along a motorway in his high powered car and well in excess of the speed limit happened to see through his car mirror the fast approach of a police patrol car.

Rightly assuming that its occupants were intent on pulling him up for speeding, he quickly picked up his stethoscope, which was conveniently to hand, and, as they drove alongside, he dangled it for the police officers to see. Taking due note, they saluted politely and drew away.

The same doctor returned an hour or two later along the same route and at the same high speed. But this time he was unaware that the same police officers had picked him up again and were once more in hot pursuit.

Just as he realised what was happening the patrol car drove past and as it did so one of the officers leant out and in his turn dangled before the doctor's eyes — a pair of hand-cuffs!

David Kelly,
Stage and Television Actor.

Of course we all know the after-dinner story where she says:

"I followed the directions on the tin, dear, so don't scream at *me*."

Louis Kentner, C.B.E.,
Concert Pianist and Composer.

The Jewish marriage broker introduces his client to the young lady selected as a prospective bride. The client finds her shockingly unattractive, and during dinner lists her shortcomings to his friend in an angry whisper. He says:

"How could you do this to me! She is monstrous, she squints, she has a beard, she is almost deformed, she . . . ."

The broker interrupts him:

"You needn't whisper. She is deaf, too."

Professor Clive Kilmister, M.Sc., Ph.D.,
Professor of Mathematics, King's College, London.

I heard my best after-dinner story in West Africa, over fifteen years ago, but it concerns the presence of mind of a professor in my own university, whose great interest was the collection of graffiti. It chanced one day that he found himself in the vicinity of Tottenham Court Road tube station and had the need to make use of the facilities provided by the municipality there.

I must emphasise that I am not speaking of the soulless place which is now to be found beneath what was once a picturesque lane, but of the dark ill-lit old place which one reached by coming out of the tube station and then descending stairs immediately in front. Anyway, it was here that he laid eyes on what he judged to be the gem that would really complete his collection.

Forgetting his mission he dashed to his rooms, which were fortunately near, to collect his camera.

Now photography has improved in recent years, so you may have forgotten the need he would have had for a tripod to support the camera for the time needed, even with a flashlight, in such a dark region.

Sensing the need for secrecy, he folded the tripod and kept it inside his trouser-leg, so giving himself a distinguished limp. On his return he found, to his joy, that no one had forestalled him and so, alone in the privacy provided by the Borough Council, he set up his tripod and camera.

I mentioned a flashlight, but in fact he had never given up his old-fashioned magnesium flare. So, when at last all was adjusted, there was a flash of light and in the enclosed atmosphere a pall of grey smoke which spread like a fog. He hastened to pack up the camera but was not quite finished when there was an anxious knocking on the door and the attendant's voice called:

"Are you all right, sir?"

Hastily replacing the tripod in his trouser-leg, the professor limped out, saying with all the cold dignity of his profession:

"Certainly. It often takes me this way."

The Hon. Lord Kincraig, Q.C.,
Senator of the College of Justice in Scotland.

Drunken voice, over the telephone:
"Is that Alcoholics Anonymous?"
"Yes. Do you wish to join?"
"No. I want to resign."

The Late Lord Kindersley, C.B.E., M.C.,
Director, Bank of England, 1947-67.

A somewhat loquacious gentleman who had been invited to reply for the guests at a large public dinner gradually became pretty well inebriated during the course of the meal, and by the time he had to get to his feet, he did so with considerable difficulty, and his speech was extremely slurred and difficult to understand. In addition to that, it went on for a very long time before he finally collapsed back into his chair.

At that stage, he turned to the gentleman sitting next to him and asked him what he thought of his speech, to which the reply came:

"Rolls Royce."

The speaker looked much perplexed and said:

"Why do you call it Rolls Royce?"

His neighbour said:

"Well, in the first place it was so silent I could hardly hear it, secondly it was extremely well oiled, and thirdly I thought it was going to last for ever."

Judge Michael King, M.A.,
A Circuit Judge; Weekend Sailor.

A keen yachtsman took his friend, whose main recreational hobby was game shooting, out for a sail in his boat. The wind changed direction suddenly and the boat was about to jibe.

The yachtsman yelled: "Duck!"

His friend stood up and said "Where?" — and was knocked overboard by the boom.

A man went into a pub.

"Good evening, sir," said the landlord, "what will you have?"

"Thank you, a large whisky," said the man.

After he had drunk it the landlord asked for payment.

"Oh, no," said the man, "I distinctly remember — you invited me to have a drink; I thought it was very kind of you."

The landlord turned to the only other customer present, who was a solicitor, and asked for support.

The solicitor placed his finger tips together and after thinking awhile said:

"He's right you know, there was an offer and acceptance — and that's a contract."

The landlord, furious, ordered the man out of his pub and never to return. A little while later the man returned.

"I thought I told you never to come back again!" said the landlord.

"Never been here in my life before," said the man.

The landlord, very puzzled but apologetic said:

"Well, all I can say is that you must have a double!"

"Thanks very much," said the man, "and I'm sure our solicitor friend here will have one too."

A father took his young son out sailing and after a very trying day during which the son had been petulant and argumentative, they returned to harbour to anchor for the night. It was pitch dark and as father manoeuvred through the shipping he told his son to go for'ard to let the anchor go.

"I don't want to hear another word from you. Stand by the anchor and when I say 'Let go' drop it over the side," he said crossly.

The son stood on the foredeck and then called to his father:

"Dad!"

"Shut up," said his father "I told you not to speak."

"But, Dad!" persisted the son.

"Will you be quiet boy! — all right, let go now!"

The son duly threw the anchor over the side.

"Is it holding?" shouted father.

Out of the darkness came another voice:

"It b-well should be! It's gone through my forehatch!"

**The Rev. Professor James Kinsley, M.A., Ph.D., D.Litt., F.B.A.,
Professor of English Studies, University of Nottingham.**

The principal of a Scottish university early in this century visited a primary school arrayed in full academic dress.

"Who am I?" he asked a class:

"A penny for the boy who knows who I am."

Silence: and then a solitary suggestion:

"Ye're God."

"No; I'm no' God; but here's tuppence."

**The Late Sir Norman Kipping, G.C.M.G., K.B.E.,
Director-General, Federation of British Industries, 1946-65.**

During an afternoon of relaxation at an international conference, to settle a bet, a race took place between the British and the Russian Ambassadors.

"The Times" reported it thus:

"A race took place between the British and the Russian Ambassadors. The British Ambassador won."

"Izvestia" reported it thus:

"A race took place between Ambassadors. The Russian Ambassador came in second. The British Ambassador was last but one."

**Sir Arthur Kirby, G.B.E., C.M.G., F.C.I.T.,
Chairman, National Ports Council, 1967-71.**

When I was General Manager of the East African Railways and Harbours I used to make frequent tours of the widespread system, not only to keep myself *au fait* with what was going on, but also, as I thought, to boost staff morale. With this in mind I made it a practice to take with me dossiers of the staff I would meet so that I could greet the stationmaster at some remote place with:

"Hallo, Chunibhai, is your wife now better and how are your two children getting on at school?"

This seemed to go down well and I was content that my scheme worked until I visited a station in the deep south of Tanganyika, on the line between Mtwara and Nachingwea, which was especially built for the ill-fated ground-nut scheme.

I greeted the stationmaster in my usual fashion, met his staff and thought I had done a successful job of staff morale boosting.

Then in came the local passenger train and soon after it left we heard the loud crash of it colliding with a lorry at the nearby level crossing. No one was hurt, so I thought it was time for me to make myself scarce and leave the stationmaster to cope.

I returned to the rail trolley in which I was travelling and the stationmaster, a large black African, put his head into the cab and, in the pleasantest way possible, said:

"Well! So long, sir, it has been a tough day, first you and then the accident."

**Air Vice-Marshal George ("Larry") Lamb, C.B., C.B.E., A.F.C.,
Chief of Staff, Headquarters No. 18 Group, Royal Air Force, 1975-78; International Rugby Referee.**

The origins of Rugby football are well known in that William Webb Ellis first picked up the ball and ran with it at Rugby School and thereby initiated the distinctive feature of the game.

What is not so well known is that after Ellis gathered the ball he ran the full length of the field jinking this way and that to avoid his opponents before throwing himself to the ground in the goal at the far end of Big Side. As he lay there panting with the ball clutched to his chest he became aware of his headmaster gazing down on him with disapproval.

"Is it a goal, sir?" gasped Ellis.

"No, son," replied the headmaster, "but it was a bloody good try!"

A very elderly rugger enthusiast decided at the age of 85 to emigrate to Australia because, he said, the growth of homosexuality appalled him.

He recalled as a boy how he heard it was punishable by hanging.

He knew as he grew older that the punishment had been reduced to a flogging. Forty years ago it had been further reduced to imprisonment; thirty years ago to a fine and now that it was no longer illegal he wished to leave the country before it was made compulsory.

**Sir Lionel Lamb, K.C.M.G., O.B.E.,
Diplomat; H.M. Ambassador to Switzerland, 1953-58.**

During the First World War an overseas Prime Minister, with a reputation for forcefulness, was being conducted on a visit to the trenches on the Western Front in response to his insistence. The British Government, however, for obvious reasons of personal safety had arranged for the visit to be made in a sector where there had been no activity for a considerable time.

On the appointed day at early dawn, the party, consisting of the guide, a British Staff Major, the Prime Minister's Private Secretary, and the Prime Minister himself, proceeded along the initial communications trenches in single file and in that order. They came to a halt after a while and the guide whispered to the Prime Minister's Private Secretary:

"Please tell the Prime Minister that we have reached the third line of trenches."

This message having been duly relayed, likewise in a whisper, the party resumed their journey until again the Major halted and asked the Private Secretary to pass on the message that they had arrived at the second line of trenches.

After moving on again the party came to its third stop, and the information that the front line of trenches had been reached was similarly communicated in whispers.

This time the Prime Minister asked the Major through his Private Secretary as before in a whisper, how far they were from the enemy.

The whispered answer was:

"About three and a half miles."

Whereupon the Prime Minister becoming a bit impatient, exploded:

"Why then have we been whispering all this time?"

The Major, who had heard this question direct, turned to the Private Secretary apologetically and whispered:

"Please tell the Prime Minister that I am very sorry but I have a bad bout of laryngitis."

As a practical demonstration of the terms "circulation of money" and "re-distribution of wealth" a business man gave each of his two teenage sons ten dollars with an injunction to use the money to best advantage and report the result at the end of a fortnight.

On due date the elder son announced that he had doubled his capital, for which he was paternally commended.

The younger son, however, admitted to having nothing left, explaining ruefully that he had lost all ten dollars to his elder brother at poker.

Sir John Lang, G.C.B.,
Secretary of the Admiralty, 1947-61; Principal Adviser on Sport to the Government, 1964-71.

The horse and mule live thirty years
And nothing know of wines or beers.
The goats and sheep at twenty die
With never a taste of scotch or rye.
The cow drinks water by the ton
And at eighteen is mostly done.
The dog at sixteen cashes in
Without the aid of rum or gin.
The cat in milk and water soaks
And then in twelve short years it croaks.
The sober, modest, bone-dry hen
Lays eggs for nogs, then dies at ten.
The animals are strictly dry
They sinless live and swiftly die.
While sinful, ginful, rum-soaked men
Survive for three score years and ten.
And some of us, though mighty few
Stay pickled till we're ninety-two.

Sir Christopher Lawrence-Jones, Bt., M.F.O.M., D.I.H.,
Central Medical Adviser, Imperial Chemical Industries Ltd.

The colonel was known to be on the mean side, and I was hardly surprised at the single pre-dinner glass of rather thin sherry offered to me.

Less expected, however, in spite of the colonel's reputation, was his behaviour when the dish containing the two deliciously grilled fresh trout arrived. One fish was conspicuously longer then the other, but, without a blush, the colonel served me with the small fish. I could not resist making some comment:

"Colonel," I said, "is this quite the thing to do?"

"What do you mean?" asked the colonel.

"Well," I replied, "if you were my guest, I would give you the large fish and keep the small fish for myself!"

"But, damn it!" said the colonel, "you've *got* the small fish, haven't you?"

Judge Paul Layton,
A Circuit Judge, formerly Deputy Chairman, Inner London Quarter Sessions, 1965-79.

Belinda Smith (or whatever name you like), aged five, was, much to her mother's concern, always telling lies. One day she came home and gave a graphic account of her meeting with a lion in the road.

After much trouble and tears she admitted that it was only a dog. Her mother told her that she must ask God's forgiveness.

After her prayers that night, asked whether she had done so, she said:

"Yes, and do you know what God said? He said, 'Don't mention it, Miss Smith, I have often made the same mistake myself'."

Late at night a police officer was checking stationary cars, and their occupants, in a quiet street. In one he saw a young man reading a book in the front seat and a girl knitting in the back seat.

Policeman: "What are you doing here?"
Young man: "Can't you see, reading a book."
Policeman: "How old are you?"
Young man: "Twenty."
Policeman: "What is she doing in the back?"
Young man: "Can't you see, knitting."
Policeman: "How old is she?"
Young man: (looking at watch)
"In eleven minutes time she will be sixteen."

The Bishop of Leeds
(The Rt. Rev. William Gordon Wheeler, M.A.).

There is a story of a company chairman who was given a ticket for a performance of Schubert's Unfinished Symphony. He couldn't go, and passed on the invitation to the company's work study consultant. The next morning the chairman asked him how he enjoyed it, and instead of a few plausible observations was handed a memorandum which read:

(a) For considerable periods the four oboe players had nothing to do. The number should be reduced, and their work spread over the whole orchestra, thus eliminating peaks of inactivity.

(b) All twelve violins were playing identical notes. This seems unnecessary duplication, and the staff of this section should be drastically cut. If a large volume of sound is really required this could be obtained through an electronic amplifier.

(c) Much effort was absorbed in the playing of demi-semiquavers. This seems an excessive refinement, and it is recommended that all notes should be rounded up to the nearest semiquaver. If this were done it should be possible to use trainees and low grade operators.

(d) No useful purpose is served by repeating with horns the passage that has already been handled by the strings. If all such redundant passages were eliminated, the concert could be reduced from two hours to twenty minutes.

If Schubert had attended to these matters, he would probably have been able to finish his symphony after all!

The Late Henry Cecil Leon, M.C.,
The Author 'Henry Cecil'; formerly County Court Judge.

Milton said: "Hard are the ways of truth."

A young naval sub-lieutenant awaiting his court martial, may well have echoed that poet's sentiments.

His ship had put into a foreign port and he had been given half a day's shore leave. There was a coal-mine near the port and he thought it would be interesting to go down it. So he obtained permission from the manager of the mine, changed into the appropriate clothes and spent most of his leave down the mine Eventually he came up, bathed and changed and, looking spick and span, started off towards his ship.

He had not gone far when he was accosted by one of his senior officers, who asked him if he would take his golf clubs and put them in the owner's cabin. He of course agreed, took the clubs and went on his way to his ship.

It so happened that when he arrived he found that the Admiral in charge of the Fleet was paying his ship a visit and was standing by the gangway.

This Admiral was a very cantankerous old man and usually took no notice whatever of officers of lowly rank, except to acknowledge their salutes.

The young man was a little dismayed at seeing the Admiral but there was nothing for it and so, first taking a quick look to see that his uniform was in order and adjusting the bag of golf clubs so as to make his general appearance as satisfactory as possible, he strode up the gangway and saluted the Admiral smartly.

For once the old man was in a benevolent mood and instead of grunting in reply to the young man's "Good evening, sir":

"Hullo, my boy," he said. "Been playing golf?"

"No, sir," replied the young man, "I've been down a coal-mine," and was immediately put under arrest for insubordination.

Major-General Peter Leuchars, C.B.E.,
General Officer Commanding Wales, 1973-76.

An English opera singer was once invited to sing at La Scala in Milan.

After completing his first aria, a particularly well-known one, he was greeted with shouts of:

"Encore!"

So he sang it again and this time the shouts were even louder.

After the third time when the same thing happened and he had taken his bow, he stepped to the front of the stage, held up his hand for silence, and said:

"Ladies and Gentleman, thank you for your wonderful reception. I am deeply touched that you should have received me in this way on my first visit to Milan. But now, if you will allow me to do so, we must continue with the opera."

At this, a man stood up at the back of the audience and shouted:

"No! No! You do notta understand. We donta want you to stop! We wanta you to go on until you getta it right!"

Sir Percy Lister, D.L.,
Engineer and Industrialist.

Jack was talking to George one day and saying how he and his wife were at daggers drawn.

"I really can't stand it," he said, "I would cut her throat, but then of course I would have to swing for that."

"Not at all," said George, "there are easier ways. You buy her a motor-bike and she'll do herself in with that."

So Jack bought his wife a fast motor-bike.

George meanwhile was away on business for a while. On his return he enquired at once about Jack's problem, only to be told that the wife was getting on marvellously with the motor-bike and having a wonderful time with it. So George suggested Jack should buy her a Jaguar and see if that would do the trick.

Again George was away for a while and returned, anxious to know how his friend's wife was getting on.

This time Jack was able to say:

"It's marvellous — the jaguar bit her head off!"

Professor Kenneth Little, M.A., Ph.D.,
Emeritus Professor of African Urban Studies, University of Edinburgh.

Many years ago, in the bygone days of colonial empire, a friend of mine was a District Commissioner in darkest Africa. He was told that the people allocated to him for administration were extremely warlike. But when he had cut his way through the rain forest he found conditions there completely peaceable. So much so, that my friend had plenty of time for his favourite pastimes — writing novels during the day and drinking whisky at night.

Headquarters had to be reassured though, because — bureaucracy being what it is — the Colonial Secretary had his annual report to prepare and the Colonial Office had in turn to account to the Treasury.

So what my friend did was what any competent civil servant would do in similar circumstances. That is to say, he had typed out in quadruplicate a very lengthy memorandum, properly numbered, and sent back in instalments by runners.

This described in detail tribal warfare, explained local campaigns and how he himself had ended a particularly bitter feud by challenging to a duel with poisoned arrows a rival tribal chieftain. My friend's own position was also made clear. Since he alone had the ear of these unruly warriors, it would only arouse suspicion and upset the delicate diplomatic equilibrium achieved if there were any intervention by fellow officials, missionaries, community developers, or anyone else at all.

And so everyone was pleased.

The people themselves because there was no further danger of outside interference. The Colonial Government because it was not called upon to take any kind of positive action. The liberals at home because at last there seemed justification for shouldering the white man's burden; and, last, but not least, my friend himself.

Not only were his creature comforts catered for until retirement, but he also received the C.B.E.; this was on the recommendation of the colonial legislature's unofficial members after my friend had modestly declined a knighthood.

Sir David Llewellyn,
Author, Journalist and Book Reviewer.

A woman went to see her solicitor, taking with her a baby in arms and four other children under the age of five.

"And what can I do for you?" he said.

"I want a divorce," she replied.

"And on what grounds?"

"Desertion, sir."

"Desertion, madam?"

He looked from her to each of the five children in turn.

"Oh, don't take any notice of them," she confided. "He really *has* deserted me. Only every now and then he comes home to apologise."

Judge David Lloyd-Jones, V.R.D.,
A Circuit Judge.

It was a small Highland kirk. The minister, one of the old school, was in full flight and was not sparing in his castigation of his flock . . .

"And there shall be much weeping and gnashing of teeth . . . ."

An old rebel, one Hamish Macgregor, whose last tooth had deserted him many years ago, grinned up at the preacher.

The challenge was accepted, and, transfixing the recalcitrant with an eagle eye, the old divine thundered:

"Do not fash yoursel', Hamish Macgregor. Teeth will be provided."

Sir Thomas Lodge, M.B., Ch.B., F.F.R., F.R.C.P., F.R.C.S.,
Consultant Radiologist, United Sheffield Hospitals, 1946-74.

A solicitor was advised by his doctor to give up all forms of alcohol as part of the treatment for his dyspepsia. Five years later, visiting the same doctor but now complaining of insomnia he was told to take a nightly tot of whisky.

The solicitor, a man of good memory, pointed out that the previous advice was to avoid alcohol completely. The doctor, a man of resource, replied:

"Ah, yes, but medicine has made great strides since those days."

Sir Norman Longley, C.B.E., D.L.,
Building Contractor; President, International Federation of Building and Public Works Contractors, 1955-57.

Members of the church committee were just finalising arrangements for the summer fête to be held on the following day.

Checking through the list of V.I.P.s someone noted that a wealthy lady in the village had not been invited.

The vicar hastily wrote a note and sent a choir-boy round with it. The lady saw the boy coming up the driveway on his bicycle and went to the door with the greeting:

"Too late, young man, I've already prayed for rain."

The Late Judge Allister Lonsdale,
A Circuit Judge.

Just after my appointment as a judge I was booking into an hotel.

The receptionist asked my name, which I gave as "Lonsdale", and she started to write in the hotel register "Mr. Lonsdale."

"Excuse me," I said, "Judge."

So she crossed out "Mr. Lonsdale" and wrote down "Mr. Judge", and said:

"I do wish you'd make up your mind what your name is."

The Hon. Ivor Lucas, C.M.G.,
H.M. Ambassador to Oman.

The Roman Emperor was enjoying a splendid afternoon's sport, watching the Christians being devoured by the lions.

Suddenly he was astonished to see one of the lions bounding up to his victim who, however, bent down and appeared to whisper something in the animal's ear, whereupon the lion turned round and slunk away.

As the Emperor watched, the same thing happened again and again; this particular Christian would say something quietly to the lion, and the latter would promptly retreat whence he came.

At last the Emperor's curiosity could stand it no longer. He sent for the Christian and promised to spare his life if only he would reveal what it was that he whispered to the lions to produce this extraordinary effect.

"Well," replied the Christian, "it's really quite simple, Your Majesty. I just say to them 'Of course, you realise that after you've dined you'll have to make a speech'."

Sir Robert Lusty,
Publisher; A Governor of the B.B.C., 1960-68.

The broad-minded vicar was invited by the broad-minded headmistress to talk to her older girls about Christianity and sex. Not wishing to compromise either his diary or his less tolerant wife he entered the engagement as "Talk to girls about sailing".

A day or so after his talk the headmistress encountered the vicar's wife.

"So very good of your husband to talk to my girls the other evening. He was quite splendid and so helpful."

"I can't imagine what he knows about it," replied the vicar's wife, "he's only done it twice and the first time he was sick and on the second occasion his hat blew off."

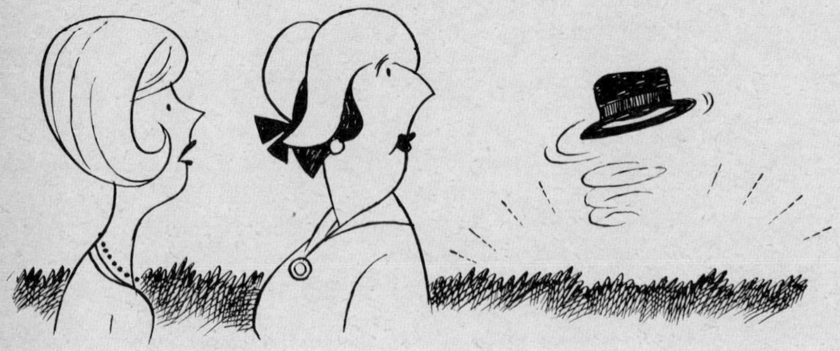

Sir Patrick McCall, M.B.E., T.D.,
Member of the Economic and Social Committee of the E.E.C., 1973-78.

The famous Mr. Justice Avory had just sentenced a hardened old rogue to 20 years' imprisonment — not uncommon in his time. He was known as the "hanging judge" somewhat unfairly — he was a great judge who looked as if he was asleep on the bench. Far from it — small and terrifying.

The old rogue said:

"But, my Lord, I shall not live that long."

Mr. Justice Avory replied:

"Well do your best, my man."

Sir Peter Macdonald, D.L., W.S.,
Industrialist.

One judge by the name of Lord Fraser wished to borrow a book one evening and for that purpose he sent his butler to the house of his colleague Lord Young.

Lord Young, who had a well-known sharp wit, said he had the book and he would be delighted to lend it to Lord Fraser.

Before handing it over, however, he wrote his name on the fly leaf and pointing to his signature as he handed the book to the butler said:

"Will you please tell Lord Fraser, that I do not in the slightest doubt his honesty. This is merely an instruction to his executors."

Air Vice-Marshal D.M.T. Macdonald, C.B.,
Director-General of Manning, Air Ministry, 1958-61.

A Scottish law lord was principal guest at a clan dinner. On rising to make the main speech of the evening he made a number of conventional remarks about "What an honour it was", "How much he enjoyed meeting, etc.", and so on, and went on to praise the excellence of the food and wine. He then continued (roughly):

"Notwithstanding your almost overwhelming hospitality, I will claim that although I may not be as sober as a judge, I am at least not as drunk as a lord."

Dr. Gordon Peter McGregor, B.A., M.Ed.,
Principal, College of Ripon and York St. John; Professor of Education, University of Zambia, 1966-70.

A prominent politician from a newly independent Pacific island territory was on his first luxury voyage on a P. & O. liner to Britain, where he was to present his credentials to Her Majesty, as Ambassador.

Very large, very black, fierce and primitive of appearance, and with a highly developed sense of humour, he entered the dining salon on the first evening and watched the steward approach him with obvious trepidation.

He scanned the ample menu for several minutes and then said in booming tones:

"No, nothing here for me, thank you — bring me the passenger list."

I was once involved in the recruitment of a night-watchman for a university in an African country in which alcohol presented very serious problems. Towards the end of one interview of what seemed a highly promising applicant, the registrar popped one of the crucial questions:

"Mr. Mukasa, if you are to be responsible for university security, we need to know a little about your personal habits. Tell me, for example, do you drink?"

There was a long pause while our would-be colleague ruminated; then he replied, with disarming candour:

"No, sir, I do not drink. I have tried drinking, but I found that I did not like it. However, if you think it is important, I will try again."

Professor Donald M. MacKay, B.Sc., Ph.D., F.Inst.P.,
Granada Research Professor of Communication, University of Keele.

Hamish had been saving up for years with the ambition of buying a car and taking a Continental holiday. His fellow labourers on the farm were as excited as he when at last the car appeared.

Hamish passed his driving test, consulted the A.A. and booked his passage; all seemed set fair for Europe. Then just the day before he was due to leave, he turned up at the farm crestfallen.

"What's up, Hamish?"

"Ach, the holiday's off."

"Off?"

"Aye. Ah'm no riskin' ma life on they roads over there. Ye see, it's this drivin' on the right. Ah thocht it wud be easy — but ah tried it last night!"

The two mice were cowering in the mousehole while the cat approached.

"Miaow . . . Miaow . . . Miaaoow . . . " they heard.

Then "Woof . . . Woof . . . Woof. . ." the sound of a furious dog, a spitting retreat, and thankful silence.

Cautiously the two mice crept out of shelter — and the cat pounced on them, remarking as he ate them up:

"I always knew it would be useful to have a second language."

Sir Hamish MacLaren, K.B.E., C.B., D.F.C.,
Director of Electrical Engineering, Admiralty, 1945-60.

The local midwife was attending the wife of Sandy, a Highland shepherd, at his cottage in a remote glen far beyond the tentacles of the hydro-board, relying on the light from a fitful candle.

Two babies were successfully delivered when the candle began to gutter.

"Get me a new candle," shouted the midwife to Sandy.

"Na, Na," replied Sandy, "I'll no' be a party to replacing the licht. It may be attractin' them."

Sir Fitzroy Maclean, Bt., C.B.E.,
Diplomat; Author; Parliamentary Under-Secretary of State for War, 1954-57.

It was at a Burns supper, and after listening to the "Address to the Haggis," the "Immortal Memory", the "Lassies", etc. for what seemed like hours, he rose to reply on behalf of the guests.

"I have often read," he said, "of people being taken to hospital suffering severely from burns. Now I know what it means."

Air Vice-Marshal Donald MacLeod, C.B., Q.H.D.S., F.D.S., R.C.S.Ed., Director of the Royal Air Force Dental Services, 1973-77.

Permissiveness has been a way of life in the Outer Hebrides for centuries. Being a product of that region my story would not be considered untypical.

North and South Uist are adjacent islands in the Outer Hebridean chain and have long been known for their religious differences — one being essentially Protestant and the other Catholic.

Hamish, a Protestant from North Uist, informed his mother of his intention to marry Morag, a Catholic from South Uist. Mother's protests came to nothing and the fine wedding took place in Glasgow, without mother, on a Saturday.

On the following Monday, Hamish presented himself back at his mother's house.

"You are supposed to be on your honeymoon," she said in consternation, whilst pouring out a struback (cuppa tea).

"Well, it's like this, mother," Hamish replied, "After a grand wedding, Morag and I went up to our room. Whilst she was getting ready for bed I was looking out the window working up a passion. Then she said: 'Hamish I've got a confession to make. I'm a virgin.' With that, I packed my bag and came straight home."

Consolingly, mother put her strong right arm around his shoulder and casually said:

"Well, Hamish, I'm glad. If she wasn't good enough for the boys of South Uist she's certainly not good enough for you!"

Judge John MacManus, T.D., Q.C., A Circuit Judge.

Irish barmaid: "I'm sorry, sir, the bar will not be open for half an hour — would you like a drink while you're waiting?"

General Sir Gordon MacMillan of MacMillan, K.C.B., K.C.V.O., C.B.E., D.S.O., M.C.,
Hereditary Chief of the Clan MacMillan; Governor and Commander-in-Chief, Gibraltar, 1952-55.

A friend of mine, who is a distinguished minister in the Church of Scotland, tells the story of an incident which occurred at a leave camp in Europe, during the 1939-45 War, where he was serving.

The R.S.M. of the camp paraded a soldier before the commanding officer on a charge of causing a disturbance. His evidence was something as follows:

"Last night I heard a disturbance in a bathroom. I went to the bathroom, knocked on the door and said, 'Who is there?'

"The answer given was, 'The Lawd Gowd Almighty'.

"Whereupon I opened the door and ascertained that this was not the case."

Lord Macpherson of Drumochter, F.R.S.A., F.R.E.S., F.Z.S.,
Banker; Chief of the Scottish Clans Association of London, 1972-74.

There was a long-winded speaker who was addressing with difficulty an unruly gathering in the Highlands. He held up his hands for silence and, when this was grudgingly given, he said:

"I am speaking not only to you but to generations yet unborn."

There was a pause and then a voice from the hall called out:

"If you don't hurry up, they will soon all be here."

A Presbyterian minister was known for his abstinence from alcoholic beverages. One evening, after a particularly good dinner with one of his elders, he was, however, persuaded to take just one small glass of cherry brandy.

After one or two had been consumed and enjoyed, his host promised to send a couple of bottles round to the manse provided the reverend gentleman acknowledged the gift in the parish magazine.

This was duly promised and the next edition of the magazine contained the following announcement:

"Your minister wishes to acknowledge and express his thanks for the most welcome gift of fruit and the spirit in which it was given."

Sir Patrick Macrory,
Barrister and Author; Director, Bank of Ireland Group, 1971-79.

In Ulster, the custom of the funeral wake is still observed.

The man had been rather ill, and his wife took him off for a month's holiday at the seaside, where they enjoyed excellent weather.

The day after he got home, he had a fatal coronary.

At his wake his friends queued up to take their leave of the departed, lying in an open coffin. One woman, having gazed fondly down at him for a minute or two, turned to the widow and said gushingly:

"Oh, doesn't he look lovely? You can see thon holiday at Portrush did him a world of good."

Major-General Reginald Madoc, C.B., D.S.O., O.B.E.,
Royal Marines (Retired).

Five men are in an aircraft. A French priest, an Irishman who is the Brain of Ireland, an Australian mountaineer, complete with rucksack, an Englishman, and the pilot.

Suddenly the pilot comes into the cabin, announces engine failure and that the aircraft is about to crash. He regrets there are only four parachutes but is sure they must all realise it is vital for him to report down below the cause of the crash. He grabs a parachute and jumps to safety.

The priest says he has a flock of five thousand souls to look after and he is a very important person to them. He grabs the second parachute and out he jumps.

Then the Brain of Ireland steps forward and says he has to represent Ireland in the Brain of the World competition next month so for the Old Country's sake he feels he has to take a parachute. So saying he jumps.

The Englishman turns to the Australian and says:

"Well, old boy, one 'chute left. What do we do now?"

"Don't worry, Cobber," says the Aussie, "there are still two 'chutes, the bloody Brain of Ireland took my bloody rucksack."

Magnus Magnusson, F.R.S.E.,
Writer and Broadcaster.

My favourite after-dinner story originally came from the "Engineers Weekly" of Denmark. It illustrates the virtues — and pitfalls — of "thinking for oneself"; and I told it myself, not after dinner but before lunch, at my Installation as Rector of Edinburgh University in the McEwen Hall, Edinburgh, on February 21, 1976 — and got away with it!

It concerned a question in physics in a degree exam at the University of Copenhagen.

The question was: "Describe how to determine the height of a skyscraper with a barometer."

One student answered as follows:

"You tie a long piece of string to the neck of the barometer, then lower the barometer from the roof of the skyscraper to the ground. The length of the string, plus the length of the barometer, will equal the height of the skyscraper."

This highly original answer so incensed the examiner that he failed the student with contumely. The student appealed to the university authorities on the ground that his answer was indisputably correct, and that he should have been given full marks.

The university appointed an impartial arbiter to decide the case, a visiting professor from the University of Washington, called Dr. Alexander Calandra. Dr. Calandra ruled that although the answer was technically correct, it did not display any noticeable knowledge of physics; and to resolve the matter, he called the student in and gave him six minutes in which to answer the question verbally in a way that showed at least a minimal familiarity with the basic principles of physics.

For five minutes there was complete silence. The student sat there frowning heavily, deep in thought. Dr. Calandra reminded him that time was running out, to which the student replied that he had several extremely relevant answers to the question, but could not make up his mind which one of them was best.

"You had better hurry up," said Dr. Calandra.

"All right then," said the student. "You take the barometer up to the roof of the skyscraper, drop it over the edge, and measure the time it takes to reach the ground. The height of the building can then be worked out in terms of the formula H = ½gt² (height equals half times gravity-time squared). But bad luck on the barometer.

"Or if the sun happens to be shining, you could measure the height of the barometer, then set it up on end and measure the length of its shadow. Then you measure the shadow of the skyscraper, and thereafter it is a simple matter of proportional arithmetic to work out the height of the skyscraper.

"But if you wanted to be highly scientific about it, you could tie a short piece of string to the neck of the barometer and swing it like a pendulum, first at ground level and then on the roof of the skyscraper, and work out the height of the building by the difference in the gravitational restoring force (T = 2π square root of *l* over *g*).

"Or if the skyscraper had an outside emergency staircase, it would be easier simply to walk up it and mark off the height of the skyscraper with a pencil, in barometer-lengths, and then add them up.

"If you merely wanted to be boring and orthodox about it, of course, you could use the barometer to measure the air-pressure on the roof of the skyscraper, compare it with standard air-pressure on the ground, and convert the difference in millibars into feet to give you the height of the skyscraper.

"But since we are constantly being exhorted to exercise independence of mind and apply scientific methods, undoubtedly the best way would be to knock on the janitor's door and say to him, 'If you would like a nice new barometer, I will give you this one if you tell me the height of this skyscraper'."

The Late Sir George Mallaby, K.C.M.G., O.B.E.,
Diplomat; High Commissioner for the United Kingdom in New Zealand, 1957-59.

I was sitting with another old man, a friend of mine, gazing with lack lustre eyes out of the windows in our club, when a very pretty girl came along, walking fast down the street. Immediately after, walking rather faster, came a personable young man in hot pursuit.

"Did you see that?" I said. "That young man, chasing that pretty girl? Do you remember how you and I used to chase pretty girls?"

Listlessly he looked at me and said:

"Yes, I remember *how* we used to chase them, but I can't remember *why*."

The Late Colonel Sir Stuart Mallinson, C.B.E., D.S.O., M.C.,
Deputy Lieutenant, Greater London, 1966-76.

Lady Mallinson was sitting at the end of a platform at an English Speaking Union meeting when she fell. The Bishop of Barking was standing by and caught her in his arms and said:

"This is the first time I have had a fallen woman in my arms."

And she said:

"This is the first time I have been picked up by a bishop."

Lord Mancroft, K.B.E., T.D.,
Chairman, British Greyhound Racing Federation; Former President, London Tourist Board.

Some while ago I went to Leningrad with a deputation from the British Tourist Authority. On the first night after our arrival the Russian travel boys threw a party in our honour. It was a fine party (they wanted a good deal from us) and by midnight we were awash in vodka.

Knowing that I had to make a speech next day I slipped away to my room, undressed, and went into the bathroom in search of Alka Seltzer. Slightly to my surprise I found an elderly Chinaman sitting in my bath washing his toes.

"Hi," I said loudly (in English, of course). To which he replied:

"Hi," equally loudly in Chinese, which, in these circumstances, sounds roughly the same.

I put on my dressing-gown, and in some confusion ran out into the corridor, and into the welcome arms of my colleagues Lord Geddes and Sir Charles Forte.

They led me back to my room explaining comfortingly that I was not drunk but had merely forgotten that in the Astoria Hotel, Leningrad, each bathroom served two bedrooms, and that unless you also locked the other door from the inside you were bound to find someone like an elderly Chinaman in your bath.

Relieved, I retired to bed, and slept the sleep of the just.

But at breakfast time next morning our interpreter, Tanya, bore down upon us with lowering brow. We asked her if ought was amiss. Indeed there was.

As a matter of fact there had been a diplomatic détente; a démarche, even. It appeared that the Deputy Chairman of the Soil Erosion Committee of the People's Republic of Outer Mongolia had been insulted in his bath by an Alcoholic Nude.

My friends tutted and clucked, but loyally did not give me away.

I'm sorry to say that I sat silent in smug content. There could be few international travel conferences, I felt, that had ever been addressed by an Alcoholic Nude, and a member of the House of Lords at that.

Professor Sir William Mansfield Cooper, LL.M.,
Professor Emeritus of Industrial Law, University of Manchester; Vice-Chancellor of the University, 1956-70.

A friend of mine, an American judge has, like many such, a jurisdiction in matrimony. He tells how, one Saturday afternoon, the chores of the week all over, he was taking it easy when a most charming young couple were shown in.

The boy, almost stifled by nervousness, said:

"Judge, we've come to ask you to marry us."

"Yes," replied the judge, "I should be delighted to do so," but went on to explain that he could not do so before Monday, because the bureau which alone could issue verification of identity was closed until then.

The young couple, utterly crestfallen, retreated to a far corner of the studio and held a whispered, but obviously agitated, conversation.

They returned in a moment or two, this time with a most determined young woman drawing along an obviously reluctant young man.

"We quite understand, Judge," she said, smiling sweetly, "we quite understand you can't *really* marry us until Monday, but do you think you could say a few words that would tide us over the weekend . . . . . .?"

Sir James Marjoribanks, K.C.M.G., Chairman, E.E.C. Committee of Scottish Council (Development and Industry).

An investment banker hired a plumber to repair a tap. He took ten minutes on the job and charged 50 dollars.

"I say," said the investment banker, "I couldn't make 50 dollars for ten minutes work."

"Nor could I," said the plumber, "when I was an investment banker."

Judge John Fitzgerald Marnan, M.B.E., A Circuit Judge, 1972-80.

Early in the Great War, Queen Mary visited a certain military hospital. She stopped at the bedside of a rifleman, who had lost a leg at the first Battle of Ypres, and asked where it had happened.

"At Vipers, M'am," said the wounded warrior.

"Ypres, my man," said The Queen.

During the conversation which followed, Her Majesty encouraged the soldier to tell the whole of his story, and on each occasion that he mentioned "Vipers" corrected him gently:

"Ypres, my man."

When the visit was over, the sister in charge of the ward enquired of her patient how he had got on with The Queen.

"Oh she was very nice," said the rifleman, "but the poor lady had terrible hiccups."

Sir Ralph Marnham, K.C.V.O., M.Chir., F.R.C.S.,
Serjeant Surgeon to The Queen, 1967-71.

A married couple bring their daughter, aged about eight, up to London to do some shopping. Among other purchases she is bought a pair of red shoes which she insists on wearing.

On the way home, going up in the elevator at Waterloo, a woman immediately in front of them suddenly, and for no apparent reason, slaps the face of the man standing next to her. There is quite a scene. At the top the ticket collector tries to calm them down but fails, other passengers join in and eventually police appear.

The parents and little girl hurry off to catch their train and, having got into their seats, start discussing this strange affair.

Suddenly the child says:

"I didn't like that woman."

"Why not?" asks the mother.

"She stepped on my new shoes," says the child, "so I gave her bottom a good pinch."

The Late Lord Marples, P.C.,
Postmaster-General, 1957-59; Minister of Transport, 1959-64.

Guests in a Cairo hotel hearing a scream in the corridor, discovered a damsel in a négligé being pursued by a gentleman who was, to put it bluntly, nude.

Later it developed that the impetuous Romeo was an English major, who was promptly court-martialed.

His lawyer won him an acquittal, however, by virtue of the following paragraph in the army manual:

"It is not compulsory for an officer to wear a uniform at all times, as long as he is suitably garbed for the sport in which he is engaged."

Sir Alan Marre, K.C.B.,
Parliamentary Commissioner for Administration, 1971-76.

An earnest temperance lady was carrying out a survey of drinking habits.

She rang the bell of a house and a bluff colonel answered.

She explained:

"I am doing a survey into people's drinking habits. If you don't object" — she was a very polite investigator — "would you mind giving me some information about yours?"

"Not at all," replied the colonel. "The fact is that I haven't had a drink since 19.45."

"Congratulations, indeed," said the lady, effusively, "that is quite a remarkable achievement."

"I know," responded the colonel, looking at his watch. "It is already 20.00 hours."

Sir Frank Marshall, M.A., LL.B.,
Chairman, Maplin Development Authority, 1973-74.

Noah Webster was the founder and compiler of "Webster's Dictionary" and was naturally a "stickler" for words — and incidentally, for his secretary.

The two of them were one day locked in fond embrace, when Mrs. Webster happened to burst into his office.

"Oh, Noah, I *am* surprised," exclaimed the good lady.

"No, my dear, you are wrong again," responded Webster. "It is *we* who are surprised. *You*, surely, are astounded."

Vice-Admiral Dennis Howard Mason, C.B., C.V.O.,
Warden, St. George's House, Windsor Castle, 1972-77.

I was brought up in Cornwall. During the war there were the same problems there (and rival ones — between adjacent villages) as there were in the rest of the country, and on one sad night a sentry of the Home Guard shot what he took to be an interloper.

At the subsequent enquiry his commanding officer said:

"Did you challenge him?"

"Yes, sir."
"What did you say?"
"Who goes there?"
"What did he say?"
"Friend, sir!"
"What did you do?"
"Shot him, sir!"
"Then why did you shoot him?"
"If it had been a real friend, he'd have said 'don't be such a silly b—' and I'd have let him pass."

The Rt. Hon. Roy Mason, M.P.,
Member of Parliament for Barnsley; Secretary of State for Northern Ireland, 1976-79.

A Member of Parliament was constantly in trouble with his wife at home and his Chief Whip in the House of Commons. The reason that he was invariably late for his meals and missing his votes in the House was the problem of his car, which kept breaking down.

So he decided to visit a car showroom. He stated that he wanted a car that was absolutely "reliable and dependable" — and explained his problem.

The showroom attendant said:

"We have just the car for you, sir," and showed him a Rolls Royce.

The M.P. had a look, opened the boot and saw a spare tyre and a kit of tools.

"What are those for?" he said. "You tell me that this car is absolutely reliable and dependable — so why a spare tyre and kit of tools?"

"Well, sir," said the attendant, "we always supply a set. Just in case!"

"Just in case?" repeated the M.P. "Where's the reliability and dependency?"

"Well, we always do," said the attendant.

But no matter how he explained, the M.P. was not satisfied. So in sheer exasperation he said:

"Look, sir, when you go into your bathroom in the morning and strip to the waist, you look into the mirror and you see" — pointing to his chest — "a red spot here and a red spot there. Now you know that you are not going to have a baby and so do I — but they are there 'just in case'!"

The Late Sir Arthur Massey, C.B.E., M.D.,
Chief Medical Officer, Ministry of Pensions and National Insurance, 1947-59.

During World War II, while on an official assignment in the U.S.A., I once had to report to our then British Ambassador in Washington, who was the head of a noble Yorkshire family.

He soon spotted that I too was a Yorkshireman but, while remarking on the fact, he warned me thus:

"Really one should never ask a man if he is of Yorkshire origin. If he is, he will tell you so in the first few minutes of conversation and if he isn't, why humiliate him?"

Professor Leonard Maunder, O.B.E., B.Sc., Ph.D., Sc.D., C.Eng., F.I.Mech.E., Professor of Mechanical Engineering, University of Newcastle-upon-Tyne.

When Sir William Thompson, later Lord Kelvin, lectured at Glasgow University, he occasionally left the actual teaching to his assistant, Dr. Day.

When Dr. Day approached the end of his lectures, he entered the lecture room one morning to find an inscription on the blackboard:

"Work while it is yet Day, for the Knight cometh when no man can work."

Successive headlines appeared in the Paris newspapers when Napoleon landed with his army on the south coast of France.

1. Corsican Fiend Lands at Marseilles.
2. Bonaparte takes Orléans.
3. Marshal Napoleon at Gates of Paris.

Lord Maybray-King, P.C., D.L.,
Speaker of the House of Commons, 1965-70; Deputy Speaker of the House of Lords.

The mean man went to stay with his friend. After dinner his friend said:

"Would you like some coffee?"
"No — tea," he replied.
Late that evening his friend asked him:
"Would you like a nightcap of whisky?"
"No—brandy," he replied.
Next morning his friend asked him:
"Would you like tea with your breakfast?"
"No — coffee," he replied.
His friend then asked:
"How would you like your eggs, scrambled or fried?"
"One fried, one scrambled," he replied.
After breakfast his friend asked him:
"Did you enjoy your breakfast?"
"No," he replied. "You scrambled the wrong egg."

Sir Peter Medawar, O.M., C.H., C.B.E., F.R.S.,
Nobel Laureate in Medicine, 1960.

When Sir Charles Sherrington, O.M., F.R.S., the world's leading neurologist, was working upon monkeys, it occurred to him to observe how his monkeys behaved when they were not under direct observation. Accordingly he tiptoed back to the room in which they were kept and looked through the keyhole, only to find another eye peering at him.

Evidently the same thought had crossed their minds.

A well-known public school was recently obliged to raise its fees by several hundred pounds per annum. All parents were notified of this by a secretary who unfortunately wrote "per anum" instead of "per annum".

One indignant parent wrote back and said he thanked the headmaster very much for the notification of the recent increase in fees, but for his part he would prefer to go on paying through the nose as usual.

Sir Anthony Meyer, Bt., M.P.,
Politician and Diplomat.

Smythe-Ffoulkes and Mainwaring-Dalrymple went to the same prep school, and took an instant and lasting dislike to one another.

The dislike deepened as they went through public school and university together, and then separated for the rest of their lives.

S-F went into the Church, and in the fullness of time became a bishop.

M-D went into the Navy, and he, in due course, became an admiral.

One day Bishop Smythe-Ffoulkes was waiting at Bath station: he had been to an investiture and was in full episcopal robes. At the far end of the platform he saw a resplendent figure in admiral's uniform. Could it be, yes it must be, that unspeakable Mainwaring-Dalrymple.

He thought for a moment. Then he went up to the admiral.

"Tell me, stationmaster," he said, "when does the next train go to London?"

The admiral, too, had recognised his former pet aversion.

"It goes in ten minutes, madam," he replied, "but in your condition I don't think you ought to be travelling."

Cliff Michelmore, C.B.E.,
Television Broadcaster and Producer.

A collection of quotations from various holiday brochures:

If this is your first visit to our hotel you are welcome to it.

You will not be likely to forget quickly your experience with us.

Situated in the shadiest part of the town, you cannot fail to remark from the window the odours of the pine trees and our swimming pool.

If you wish for breakfast, lift the telephone, ask for room service, and this will be enough for you to bring your food up.

On gala nights the chef throws his best dishes, and all water used in cooking has been passed by the manager personally.

If your wife needs something to do, she should apply to our suggestive head porter, but all of our staff are courteous, and to ladies too attentive.

We would very much like to have relations with you, and we will be most happy to dispose of all your clients.

Sir George Middleton, K.C.M.G., F.R.S.A.,
Diplomat; H.M. Ambassador to the United Arab Republic, 1964-66.

There was once a very hungry raffish Tom Cat. Although he was ugly and torn and scarred the Pussy Cats adored him for his rough forthright approach. But he kept everyone awake for miles around.

The neighbours decided something had to be done. One night he disappeared. He had been kidnapped and sent away to be "doctored".

The Pussies mourned him for many a long moonlit night.

Then suddenly a new fat silky cat turned up in Tom's old haunts. Yes, it was Tom himself! A thousand amorous mewings were heard. But Tom was unmoved.

Stalking proudly among his old loves he was heard to say:

"Sorry girls, but I'm only a consultant now."

Ian Mikardo, M.P.,
Chairman, International Committee of the Labour Party, 1973-78.

An elderly duke was the guest of honour at the annual dinner of his County Conservative Association. The following morning he was walking in the High Street of the county town, and he ran into an old friend who said:

"I'm so sorry I couldn't get to the county dinner last night. How was it?"

"Tell you what," said the duke, "let's slip into the club, and you shall buy me a small Madeira and I'll tell you all about the dinner."

Five minutes later they were seated in deep armchairs in the smoking room of the club, each sipping his Madeira and nibbling at a thin biscuit.

"Well, Arthur," said the duke, heaving a deep sigh, "I'll tell you about last night's dinner. If the melon had been as cold as the soup was, and if the soup had been as warm as the claret was, and if the claret had been as old as the chicken was, and if the chicken had been as young as the waitress was, and if the waitress had been as willing as the Duchess was, I'd have had a jolly good evening!"

Sir Richard Miller, M.A.,
Chairman, Arthritis and Rheumatism Council, North-West Region.

Two aged Chelsea Pensioners were reminiscing about their experiences in the Boer War.

First Pensioner to the other: "George, do you remember them pills they used to give us — you know, them pills which they told us would help us to keep our minds off the girls?"

George: "Aye, come to think of it, I do."

First Pensioner: "Well, do you know I think mine are beginning to work."

An Irishman on a visit to Liverpool meets a friend.

The friend: "Hullo, Paddy, when did you come over?"

Paddy: "Yesterday."

The friend: "And did you come by sea or air?"

Paddy: "I don't know, you see my wife bought the tickets."

The vicar was rather taken aback when he noticed that a girl in his congregation bowed her head every time the devil was mentioned, so he stopped her on her way out of the church and asked her why she did it.

The girl replied: "Well, vicar, politeness costs nothing and you never know."

Hikers from Aberdeen, caught by a snowstorm in the Cairngorms, took refuge in a hut for the night.

Next morning a search party with Red Cross personnel set out. They saw the hut and knocked on the door.

Voice from inside: "Who's there?"

"The Red Cross."

Voice from inside: "We've already given, thank you."

Vice-Admiral Sir Charles Mills, K.C.B., C.B.E., D.S.C.,
Commander-in-Chief Plymouth, 1967-69; Lieutenant-Governor and C.-in-C. Guernsey, 1969-74.

Many years ago there was a complaint at Plymouth by Lord Mount Edgcumbe that matelots were bathing in the harbour from his private steps. There were also complaints by the citizens that men were bathing naked.

A young lieutenant, R.N., was told to compose a suitable notice.

After long thought he produced and erected the following:

"Nobody is allowed to bathe from these steps without bathing trunks except the Earl of Mount Edgcumbe and the Commander-in-Chief."

The Hon. Sir Alan Mocatta, O.B.E.,
Judge of the High Court of Justice (Queen's Bench Division).

A wife gives her husband two ties for Christmas and he comes down to breakfast wearing one on Christmas morning.

"Oh, my dear! Didn't you like the other one?"

Major-General Viscount Monckton of Brenchley, C.B., O.B.E., M.C., D.L.,
Chief of Staff, Headquarters, British Army of the Rhine, 1965-67.

This concerns a senior minister who was known to drink too much.

Attending a reception in a South American country he walked over to a figure in red when the music started and asked for a dance.

The answer was a "NO" for three reasons:

"First, you are drunk, secondly the music is the National Anthem and finally I am the Cardinal Archbishop!"

Patrick Moore, O.B.E.,
Astronomer, Author and T.V. Presenter.

Did you know that the first two astronauts who landed on the Moon were British?

Naturally, one went out to look for a lunar pub, but when he came back he looked very glum.

"Well," said his companion, "any luck?"

The pioneer shook his head.

"Useless. I found a pub, but it was no good. No atmosphere!"

Robert Morley, C.B.E.,
Actor and Dramatist.

A man was lonely and bought a budgerigar on the understanding it would talk to him.

Disappointed by the bird's lack of conversation, he complained to the pet shop proprietor, who advised the purchase of a mirror, and when this failed to make his feathered friend converse, suggested some cuttle-fish wedged between the bars.

After this, the man returned daily to the shop equally disappointed, and was advised to buy a swing, and then a ladder, and finally a bell to give the little bird a purpose in life.

"You will find," said the pet shop proprietor, "once he has given himself a swing, loosened his beak with the cuttle-fish, climbed the ladder and rung the bell, he is sure to say something."

A week later the man returned triumphant.

"It worked," he said. "He swung, swallowed, climbed, rang the bell and then fell backwards on to the floor of the cage with his feet in the air."

"Did he say anything?"

"Yes, just before he expired he said, 'Did no one tell you about *bird seed*?'."

The Late Lord Morris of Borth-y-Gest, C.H., P.C., C.B.E., M.C.,
A Lord of Appeal, 1960-75.

A man became involved in some litigation in the High Court. All his friends told him that as difficult and important points would arise it would be wise for him to obtain legal advice and to be represented at the hearing. He thought otherwise. Without any professional help he conducted his own case.

When he came to his final speech he concluded with an eloquent flourish:

"I am aware, My Lord, that there is an old adage which says that he who is his own lawyer hath a fool for a client: yet such, My Lord, is my respect for this Court that it is with confidence that I leave my case in your hands."

There were reasons which unavoidably prevented him from remaining in Court to hear the judgement. He left some money with the usher to pay for a telegram which he asked might be sent to him to tell him the result of the case.

An hour or two later a telegram arrived. With trembling hands he opened it. It read:

"Old adage affirmed — with costs."

The Late Sir Philip Morris, K.C.M.G., C.B.E., M.A., LL.D., Educationalist; Vice-Chancellor, University of Bristol, 1946-66.

The visit of the distinguished professor for his special lecture had come to an end. His professorial host, out of consideration for the lameness of his guest, had got him to the station in very good time for his train. They sat together on a sunny bench in the wide part of the curved platform while they waited for the train to come in.

Conversation did not flag, each of them having a quiverful of well prepared extempore darts, sharp but in the name of humanity not poisoned, ready to launch into the urbane quarrel which, after more than twenty years, they still continued. Time-pressed if all the darts were to be delicately launched — and what a shame it would be to waste even one of them!

In due course the train crept slowly round the curve of the platform and came imperceptibly to its brief halt. Neither of the professors noticed its advent but both were galvanised into activity by the guard's whistle and the banging of a few doors.

Both of them jumped up and made what haste they could toward the now gently moving train. One broke into a run and jumped on board while the other was intercepted by the platform inspector who remonstrated with him for daring to try to break one of the company's by-laws, and threatened prosecution.

But the professor brushed aside the remonstrations remarking in acid tones:

"Never mind that. That man came to see me off."

Sir Brian Morton, F.R.I.C.S.,
Chairman, Londonderry Development Commission, 1969-73; Chairman, Harland and Wolff, 1975-80.

I was presenting the prizes on speech day at an English school. After the ceremony the boys spontaneously started singing "When Irish Eyes Are Smiling," obviously as a compliment to me. The singing was untuneful, out of key and even raucous.

I noticed a lady in the platform party putting her handkerchief to her eye, to wipe away a tear. Thinking she had become emotionally overcome, I put my hand on her shoulder and said:

"Are you Irish?"

"No," she replied, "I'm a music teacher."

Sir Charles Mott-Radclyffe, D.L.,
Member of Parliament for Windsor, 1942-70; High Sheriff of Norfolk, 1974-75.

During some dredging operations in the Fen country along the River Ouse, the owners of a row of bungalows each with a "privy" in the back garden near the water's edge had begun to get nervous as the banks gradually subsided. One day at lunch time, one of the bungalow owners was distinctly angry when his privy collapsed into the water.

Suspecting his small boy of a mischievous act, he asked him outright:

"Did you push our privy into the river at lunch time to-day?"

The small boy denied this, albeit with a somewhat shifty eye.

"Look here, sonny," said his father, "you are not looking me straight in the face. Do you ever learn any history at school?"

"Yes, father."

"Have you ever heard of George Washington?"

"Yes, father."

"Did you know that George Washington, as a small boy, cut down his father's favourite cherry tree in the garden and when confronted by his father he owned up and told the truth and as a reward for telling the truth, his father did not beat him?"

"No, father, I did not know about that."

"Did you know that George Washington ultimately became President of the United States and went down in history as the man who never told a lie?"

"No, father."

"Well, let's run through this again. Who knows what the future might hold for you if all your life you stick to the truth? You might be able to buy a Mini Mackintosh and go to the Scilly Isles for a holiday and become Prime Minister of England. Did you or didn't you push our privy into the Ouse at lunch time today?"

The boy confessed that he had, and his father took off his belt and gave him a good thrashing, after which the boy wept copiously.

"This is very unfair, father," he said. "I only owned up and told the truth about the privy because you told me that George Washington wasn't beaten by his father when he owned up and told the truth about the cherry tree."

"Yes," replied his father, "but there is one essential difference between George Washington's father and me, which I forgot to mention. George Washington's father wasn't sitting on the cherry tree when George Washington cut it down."

Air Vice-Marshal Leslie Moulton, C.B., D.F.C., F.R.S.A.,
Air Officer Commanding, No.90 (Signals) Group, Royal Air Force, 1969-71.

The night was clear and starlit as the jumbo jet ploughed its way across the Atlantic at 35,000ft. en route for London Airport.

Two hours or so out from New York the captain spoke on the intercom:

"I have had to close down No. 1 engine; sorry about this, we shall be about 20 minutes late at Heathrow."

All was quiet for the next few minutes and the passengers went on sipping their free drinks in the first-class compartment until the captain spoke again:

"Sorry everybody, trouble with No. 2 engine; I have had to shut it down and we shall be about 40 minutes late in London."

Half an hour later more trouble was apparent and the captain, without the slightest hint of concern in his voice, spoke up again:

"This really is getting embarrassing; No.3 engine has cut out; I'm afraid we're going to be a couple of hours late on this run."

The only comment from among the passengers came from an Irishman as he accepted his seventh whisky from the stewardess:

"Let's hope we don't lose any more engines or we'll be up here all night!"

The Late Sir Francis Mudie, K.C.S.I., K.C.I.E., O.B.E.,
Diplomat; Governor of West Punjab, 1947-49; Member of the Commission on the Constitution of the Isle of Man, 1958.

A parish minister in Scotland about, say, one hundred years ago decided that his flock needed pulling together and reminding of the awful penalties which awaited unrepentant sinners. Accordingly he preached them a sermon, setting forth in detail their backslidings, and concluding:

"When the great day comes and you see the flames of hell rushing up to catch you, you will cry: 'Lord, Lord, we didna' ken, we didna' ken', and the Lord in His infinite compassion will say:

" 'Ye ken noo, ye ken noo'."

Richard Murdoch,
Stage, Film, Radio and Television Actor.

This after-dinner story was told at a Stage Golfing Society dinner at the Savoy Hotel by my old friend Naunton Wayne — an incomparable raconteur.

He recounted how he had a fire in his bedroom and the insurance company were unwilling to compensate for the damage as they said he had obviously gone to bed drunk and had been smoking and set fire to the bed through carelessness.

His reply was that in the first place he had been stone-cold sober and in the second place the bed was already on fire when he got into it.

Peter Murray, C.M.G.,
Diplomat; H.M. Ambassador to Ivory Coast, Upper Volta and Niger, 1970-72.

Before a dance at Balmoral Castle, the company were waiting for The Queen. The Queen Mother was chatting to the Colonel of the Scots Guards;

one of his subalterns had just won a country dancing competition and she would like him to partner her for the first reel.

The Colonel beckoned to the young man, who was standing by the door, and was taken aback when he took no notice. He walked over and spoke sharply, but the boy explained, blushing, that he was to partner The Queen herself.

The Queen arrived, the band struck up and the reel began. As The Queen Mother passed the subaltern she smiled, tapped him with her fan and whispered:

"Snob!"

Lieut.-Colonel Sir Edmund Neville, Bt., M.C.,
Commander, Light Infantry Training Centre, 1941-44.

A young woman at her first cocktail party was overheard to say to her escort:

"I have had only tee martoonis; I'm not so drunk as thinkle peop I am but I fool so feelish and the drunker I sit the longer I get."

Viscount Newport,
Landowner.

A young Irish girl goes to church for confession, and says to the priest:

"Oh Father, Father, I have sinned grievously. On Monday night I slept with Sean. On Tuesday night I slept with Patrick, and on Wednesday night I slept with Mick. Oh Father, Father, what shall I do?"

"My child, my child," replied the priest, "go home and squeeze the juice from a whole lemon and drink it."

"Oh, Father, Father, will this purge me of my sin?" she asked.

"No child, but it will take the smile off your face."

Sir Rex Niven, C.M.G., M.C.,
British Colonial Service, Nigeria, 1921-54; Speaker, Northern House of Assembly, 1952-60.

Two distinguished gentlemen were driving to an appointment in a part of the country unknown to them. After a while they realised that they were lost and decided to stop and ask the way. As fate would have it, the first human being they saw was not very helpful.

He had never heard of their destination nor of places they mentioned that might be adjacent to it. Finally and unwisely, the man driving said in exasperation:

"Well, thank you very much, but I can't say you seem to know much."

The yokel said: "Ah, but maybe I knows more than thee; thee be lost, but I knows where I be."

Lord Noel-Baker, P.C.,
Author and Statesman; Nobel Peace Prize, 1959.

In the days of the private railway companies Sir Thomas Beecham, the famous conductor, was travelling once to an important concert in a first-class non-smoking compartment. Shortly, an expensive looking lady in the corner opposite leaned forward, opened her handbag and said:

"You will not object if I smoke?"

Sir Thomas, with great courtesy replied:

"No, madam, and you will not object if I am sick."

Greatly offended, the lady said:

"I do not think you know who I am. I have some influence on this line; I am one of the Directors' wives."

And Sir Thomas said:

"Madam, if you were the Director's *only* wife I should still be sick."

Denis Norden, C.B.E.,
Scriptwriter and Broadcaster.

I'm told that in India today, as well as in Scandinavia and several American states, they have inaugurated a telephone service for birth control advice.

In other words, just by dialling three figures — like you do for weather reports or the Wimbledon results — you can be told over the telephone the most appropriate birth control system to adopt right at the moment when the assistance is most necessary.

Isn't that impressive? Mind you, do you know what I find the most intriguing thing about it? The thought that twenty years from now there will be people walking the earth who owe their entire existence to a wrong number.

**The Rev. Dr. E.R. Norman,
Dean of Peterhouse, Cambridge.**

When the late Edward Welbourne was Master of Emmanuel College, Cambridge, he used to undertake all the correspondence relating to the admission of undergraduates himself. It was from him, therefore, that as a schoolboy I received a letter, in reply to an application I had made to his college, suggesting that my qualifications were such as to make it unlikely that I would ever be good enough either for his, or for any other college. In view of my academic record up to that time, that was a very fair comment.

However, fortune smiled upon my labours and a dozen or so years later I met Welbourne at a feast in Jesus College, where I was a tutor at the time.

Perhaps rather impertinently, I actually reminded him of his earlier assessment.

"Very interesting," said the great man, "and what do you do now?"

I replied: "I am a Fellow of this College."

"Ah well," he said, "I was right, then, wasn't I?"

The Late Lieut.-General Lord Norrie, G.C.M.G., G.C.V.O., C.B., D.S.O., M.C., Governor, South Australia, 1944-51; Governor-General, New Zealand, 1952-57; Chancellor, Order of St. Michael and St. George, 1960-68.

I attended a dinner recently where the evils of drink were to be discussed.

The speaker, after the usual anti-drink speech, exemplified his reasons by showing the guests a live worm placed in a glass of water and another live worm put into a glass of whisky and water.

Half an hour later he showed off the two glasses. The worm in the water was wriggling strongly but the worm in the whisky was dead as a door nail.

He turned round to his audience and said:
"Now what is the moral of this demonstration?"
A reply came quickly:
"If you don't want to get worms, drink whisky."

Sir Arthur Norrington, M.A., J.P.,
Secretary to the Delegates, Oxford University Press, 1948-54; President, Trinity College, Oxford, 1954-70; Vice-Chancellor, Oxford University, 1950-52.

A man who unexpectedly gave £100,000 to an appeal was asked how he was able to give so much.

"A little of it," he said, "is due to hard work, a little more to frugal habits, and £98,000 to a recent legacy from a rich uncle."

Professor Alexander Nove, F.B.A.,
Professor of Economics, University of Glasgow.

When Marx died, he found himself facing St. Peter, who said:

"Name?"

"Karl Marx."

"*The* Karl Marx? Dialectical materialism and all that?"

"Yes."

"Well in that case, we will give you a choice. Where would you like to go?"

Marx replied: "I am in some difficulty, never having seen either place."

"Just go and have a look," said St. Peter. "Hell is down there, try that first."

So Marx went down there, looked over the wall, and saw, sitting on a sofa with a luscious unclad blonde on his lap, someone looking remarkably like Karl Marx.

"Well," he said to himself, "so that is hell? What can heaven be like?"

So he went to have a look. And there, as he looked over the wall, he saw, sitting on a sofa, with a luscious unclad blonde on his lap, someone looking remarkably like Karl Marx.

He returned to St. Peter.

"I really do not mind where I go, I see no difference."

"No difference?"

"None at all."

"You, a master of dialectical materialism, can see no difference?"

"There is none."

"But," said St. Peter, "there is a fundamental difference. Down there *she* is being punished. Up here, *you* are being rewarded."

Admiral Sir William O'Brien, K.C.B., D.S.C.,
Commander-in-Chief Western Fleet, 1970-71.

The United States was still a non-belligerent. Lend-Lease was in full operation at Government level and, at the private level, food parcels and bundles of clothing flowed to Britain.

The glamorous young Rear Admiral was guest of honour at a large dinner party where he was to express his country's thanks to the people of Washington for their generosity.

He found difficulty concentrating upon his neighbour's conversation. His eyes kept snapping back to that beautiful creature opposite; that face, that figure, that plunging neckline — most distracting.

Eventually the girl leant towards him and said:

"Admiral, to relieve you of any further anxiety, let me explain. Yes, the 'V' is for Victory but the bundles are not for Britain."

The Late Sir Alwyne Ogden, K.B.E., C.M.G.,
Diplomat; Consul-General, China, 1941-48.

Do dreams "come true"? Well, I can vouch for at least one that did follow exactly as the dreamer had foretold.

In 1945, soon after World War II came to an abrupt end, I was flown into Shanghai, as Consul-General, to get back the large British community out of the internment camps and back to their normal life. This was a very full-time job and I was not much pleased when I was asked to go to Tokyo for a conference of Far Eastern Consuls-General. I was able to plead that I just could not get there because there were no ships or planes then available. Then the arrival in Shanghai of an Air Vice-Marshal on his way from Singapore to Washington via Tokyo altered the situation — though I did not at once realise this.

He had asked me to find accommodation for himself and his air crew and also to arrange, if possible, for him to meet some of the Americans he had known during the War. For this meeting I arranged a cocktail party to which I also asked a few senior British officials, including the captain of a cruiser that happened to be in port at the time. The latter when he saw the Air Vice-Marshal (whom he had never met before or even heard of until he got my invitation) said:

"Oh, I'm so pleased to see you alive! I dreamed last night that I saw your plane crash in Japan!"

At the time they were unable to discuss it further, owing to the arrival of other guests, but when they met at dinner at my house afterwards he went into details.

"Oh, yes it was a most vivid dream. I saw your plane make a crash landing on a little beach in an island off Japan in most frightful weather — a snowstorm in fact — as it was getting dark —"

"Could you see who were in the plane?"

"Yes. Besides the Service crew there were three people in 'civvies', two men and a woman." The Air Vice-Marshal laughed and said:

"Well, that lets me out then. I'm not taking any passengers," and they turned to other topics.

But that was not the end of it. Soon afterwards the Air Vice-Marshal was called to the phone and, as he passed me on his way back, said:

"That was Seymour Berry" (now Lord Camrose) "whom I had given a lift to Shanghai; he now wants to go on to Tokyo."

Shortly afterwards my Vice-Consul on duty sent a note to say that the Ambassador had heard of the Air Vice-Marshal's arrival and suggested that I might get him to take me to Tokyo as the Foreign Office were interested in the conference. I asked him across the table and, after a brief hesitation (which I did not understand until later), he agreed.

Finally, towards the end of dinner, the Vice-Consul sent in a further note to say that Tokyo asked if I could bring a secretary as they were very short-handed and he had made inquiries and one of our girls, Dorita B, was willing to go. When I asked the Air Vice-Marshal he was even more hesitant (realising that this would make up the "two men and a woman" of whom the captain had spoken), but of course he agreed.

We set off two days later on a bright, frosty morning and we made such good progress that we expected to be in Tokyo soon after noon. When we were off the south-east tip of Japan the Air Vice-Marshal thought that we could afford to make a slight diversion to fly over Hiroshima, where the first atomic bomb had been dropped.

So we turned north — and then our troubles began.

Hitherto we had been flying at the height of a few hundred feet over a sunlit sea. Now we ran into cloud which got thicker the further north we went. If we rose higher to get above the clouds, breathing became difficult and the strain on our ears painful (as the plane was not, of course, pressurised), and when we got to a height of over 10,000 feet, it was positively dangerous because, there being no oxygen on board, the pilot and navigator could not think clearly or quickly enough.

We could not make straight for Tokyo because of the central massif (especially Mt. Fuji) and when we came down off the north coast and tried to approach the capital from the north-east, we found ourselves in a different, almost Arctic, world (the south of Japan being tempered by the equivalent of the Gulf Stream). At last it became clear that we could not reach Tokyo and had missed Niigata, where there was an American airfield, and — to save our lives — must make a landing on any piece of land that appeared to be long enough to take us.

Well — thanks to the skill of our pilot — it was not a crash landing (though abrupt enough to be most unpleasant) but otherwise just as the captain had seen in his dream and had described it:

". . . . a beach . . . . on a little island off Japan . . . . in frightful weather . . . a snowstorm . . . . as it was getting dark . . . ."

Lord O'Neill of the Maine, P.C.,
Prime Minister of Northern Ireland, 1963-69.

A man was very worried about his wife's state of mind, so he went to see a psychiatrist.

The following conversation ensued:

Husband: "The trouble about my wife is that she thinks she is a horse."

Psychiatrist: "I am afraid that if she thinks she's a horse, it will be very expensive to cure her."

Husband: "Have no worry, doctor, have no fear; she's just won the Kentucky Derby!"

The Late Professor C.W. Ottaway, Ph.D., F.R.C.V.S.,
Emeritus Professor of Veterinary Science, University of Bristol.

The professor was addressing an 8 a.m. lecture.

"I've found that the best way to start the day is to exercise for five minutes, take a deep breath of air and then finish with a cold shower. Then I feel rosy all over."

A sleepy voice from the back of the room:

"Tell us more about Rosy."

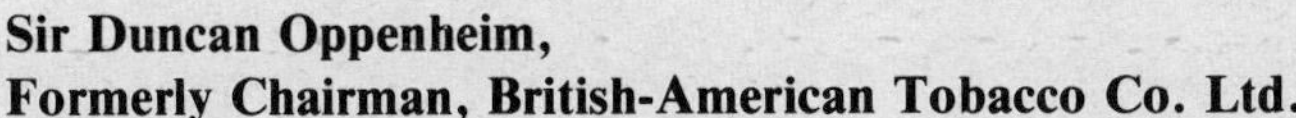

Sir Duncan Oppenheim,
Formerly Chairman, British-American Tobacco Co. Ltd.

An Eastern diplomat taking leave of Lord Lansdowne said:

"My Lord, I must not cockroach on your time any further."

The diplomatic Lord Lansdowne replied:

"Oh! your Excellency, do not hurry away. Before you go I wish to congratulate you on the command of the English language that you have acquired during your short stay. I am sure your Excellency would not take it amiss, however, if I point out that the correct word is not 'cockroach' but 'encroach'."

"My Lord," replied the Ambassador, "forgive me, but I am addressing you and therefore I use the word 'cockroach' whereas if I had been addressing her ladyship I would then be correct to use the word 'hencroach'."

John Eryl Owen-Jones, C.B.E., J.P., D.L.,
Clerk of the Peace for Caernarvonshire and Clerk of the County Council, 1956-74.

The Bishop of Bangor was summoned to the presence of Henry VIII to be catechised, and on pain of beheading to give the right answers.

Now, the bishop, not being a learned man, and fearing that his lack of learning would cost him his head, spoke to his brother, a friar at the Dominican Friary of Bangor, who bore a strong facial likeness to the bishop, and who anyway was a learned man.

"Leave it to me," said the friar. "The King has never seen us before; I will impersonate you and appear before the King."

And so it came to pass.

"I have three questions, my Lord Bishop," said the King, "and on pain of beheading, you must answer them correctly.

"First, how deep is the ocean?"

"My Liege King, I will make answer, the ocean is as deep as a stone's throw."

The King thought this was as good an answer as any and let it pass.

"My next question is this: Who was the greatest man who walked the earth?"

"I suppose you expect me to say it was you, Your Majesty, but I must say the greatest man was Jesus Christ."

The King, somewhat grudgingly, accepted this was so, but with a stern warning put his last question.

"Be you not over-confident, my Lord Bishop, you are a reader of books, then read my mind; what am I thinking at this moment, tell me?"

"My Lord, I am so relieved, I can answer that easily — you're thinking I'm the Bishop of Bangor. I'm not — I'm his brother."

Sir Antony Part, G.C.B., M.B.E.,
Permanent Secretary, Department of Industry, 1974-76.

Sir Winston Churchill (at a diplomatic reception where he was served a very weak whisky and soda):

"My boy, which did you put in first — the whisky or the soda?"

Attendant (anxious to show that he knew what he was doing):

"Oh, sir, I put in the whisky first."

Churchill: "That's very good. Then no doubt I shall come to it in due course!"

Small boy: "Grandfather, were you in the Ark?"

Grandfather (very grumpy): "No, I was *not* in the Ark."

Small boy (with relentless logic): "Well, why weren't you drowned then?"

Sir John Partridge, K.B.E.,
Chairman, Imperial Group Ltd., 1964-75.

Particularly when one is about to open one's mind to a collection of fellow human beings, it is worth recalling that over-ambition is a pit of human frailty into which any one of us is liable to fall. I recall a sad and cautionary tale that illustrates this.

A candidate for Congress in one of the Southern States of U.S.A. had taken great pains over the opening speech of his campaign. He duly delivered it in the largest hall in his home town. It fell with a thud sufficient to split the floor.

Alone in his subsequent misery, he summoned a faithful camp-follower and the following dialogue ensued:

Candidate: "Ed, you bin listenin'?"

Ed: "I bin listenin', Joe."

Joe: "What's wrong, Ed?"

Ed: "I tell you. Three things wrong, Joe. One, you read your speech. Two, you don't read good. Three, what you got there ain't fittin' sayin'."

The Late Michael Pattrick, C.B.E., F.R.I.B.A., A.A.Dipl., Principal, Central School of Art and Design.

At a marketing conference dinner the talk was about the difficulty of language and communications in international trade.

The director of an engineering firm said that his export director was astonished to receive an order from Russia for a thousand water sheep. A representative was dispatched to investigate.

The actual requirement was for hydraulic rams.

Vice-Admiral Sir Arthur Pedder, K.B.E., C.B., Commander, Allied Naval Forces, Northern Europe, 1957-59.

My father, Sir John Pedder, who was an eminent pillar of the Home Office, once had occasion, when I mentioned Cabinet Minutes (in private of course) to say:

"What a stupid innovation! That fellow Hankey introduced them during the Kaiser's War."

I asked how they knew what they had decided, to which he replied:

"They didn't. When I was P.A. to the Home Secretary I well remember being sent for after a Cabinet Meeting and told, 'I can't remember what we decided about so and so, but I'll tell you what we are going to do about it'."

Sir Rudolf Peierls, C.B.E., F.R.S., M.A., D.Sc., D.Phil., Wykeham Professor of Physics, University of Oxford, 1963-74.

An ambulance arrived at a large maternity hospital in Moscow, and on the stretcher was a man, who showed the usual symptoms of labour pains. The receiving doctor asked in amazement how this had happened, and the patient answered in a feeble voice:

"Well, doctor, this is a long story, but it all started with doing the dishes."

An architect, whose designs were always accepted by the commission in charge of buildings, was asked by a less successful colleague for the secret of his success.

"Very simple," he said. "When I design a building, I put in a prominent place on it two very ugly dogs. When members of the commission object I insist that they are essential for the artistic balance of the design, which would be ruined without them. After prolonged argument I finally agree to remove the dogs, and the commission then pass the design."

One of my teachers, Professor Erhard Schmidt, a very distinguished mathematician, told his class one morning about the problem he had the day before on returning home.

When he wanted to open the door to his flat, the key would not fit, and there was a stranger's name on the door. He thought he might have mistaken the floor, and tried the one above and the one below, with no more success. So he went down to the porter and asked:

"Does not Professor Schmidt live here?" to get the answer:

"No, sir. He moved yesterday."

Sir Anthony Percival, C.B.,
Under-Secretary, Board of Trade, 1949-58; President, Berne Union of Export Insurance Organisations, 1966-68.

The chairman of the meeting spoke at considerable length and rather over insistently. It suddenly struck him that he did not perhaps have the sympathy of the other members as much as he had hoped.

He interrupted himself and asked one member of the committee who was better known to him than the rest:

"George, you look as though you think I have been talking too much."

George replied: "Mr. Chairman, the thought would never cross my lips!"

Michael Pertwee,
Playwright and Screenwriter.

There's this rich bachelor, lives alone with a cat, which he adores, and looked after by a faithful manservant.

He goes off on holiday to the Carlton in Cannes leaving the manservant in charge of pussy. On arrival at the Carlton he finds a telegram awaiting him which states baldly:

"Pussy dead."

He is deeply shocked, returns to London where he berates his manservant for tactlessness and insensitivity. He says:

"Look, Wilkins, if anything similar should ever occur, you should send a telegram saying: 'Pussy's on the roof and won't come down'; then wait a few hours before sending a second telegram saying: 'Pussy fell off roof, badly injured'; then wait a few more hours before sending a third telegram saying: 'Regret pussy is dead'. That way it lessens the shock."

The manservant takes note of this and apologises.

The next year the man went off on holiday as usual.

On his arrival at the Carlton he found a telegram awaiting him which said:

"Your mother's on the roof and won't come down."

The Late Sir Charles Petrie, Bt., C.B.E., M.A., F.R.Hist.S., Historian and Editor.

A newly-elected Mayor of a small borough was proposing the loyal toast, and proceeded to elaborate upon The Queen's virtues at some length.

After the function was over the Town Clerk politely told him that in such circumstances it was customary to propose the toast and leave it at that.

So the next time a similar situation arose the Mayor said:

"Ladies and Gentlemen, The Queen; and the Town Clerk tells me the less I say about her the better."

Professor Owen Hood Phillips, Q.C., J.P., D.C.L., M.A., LL.M., Legal Writer; Formerly Dean of the Faculty of Law, University of Birmingham.

An English bishop was making a tour of some schools in a rural district in Africa. He asked a little black boy whether he liked being at school.

"Yes, sir," answered the boy, "because if you haven't got education you've sure got to use your brains."

An American millionaire was married to a woman who had a great ambition to be an operatic prima donna, but unfortunately she was not very good at singing. For many years the millionaire hired large concert halls and orchestras to enable her to sing in public, though audiences were thin and the critics unfavourable.

When at length she decided it was time to retire, she said:

"People may say I couldn't sing, but they can't say I didn't."

An Irishman was giving evidence in an English case, and the judge formed the strong impression that the witness was not telling the truth.

"What happens in your country," the judge asked him, "to a witness who tells lies?"

To which the Irishman replied:

"Sure, your Honour, I think his side usually wins."

In the earlier part of this century a certain bishop had been in office for very many years. His dean, who incidentally had held office nearly as long, once remarked:

"The dear Bishop has every Christian virtue save that of resignation."

The Late Sir George Pickering, F.R.S., M.D., F.R.C.P.,
Master of Pembroke College, Oxford, 1968-74.

I once had to write a report on medical education. We were urged that teachers should teach fundamental principles, not facts.

As I tried to write, I wondered what a fundamental principle was. I came to the conclusion that it was the same as basic prejudice, but that one was O.K., the other was not. It was in fact the hypothesis with which one approached a new set of data.

It was some years later that I came across a story that illustrated this.

A little boy, who was the only child of parents who lived on the north side of the Ulster/Eire border, was asked to go for a picnic with a little girl, who was the only child of parents on the south side of the border.

It was a sunny, hot July day and they picnicked by a river. The children took all their clothes off and played in the water.

When the little boy got home his mother said to him:
"Johnny, was it interesting?"
He replied: "Yes, Mummy, it was fascinating. I never knew before what a big difference there is between Protestants and Catholics."

The Late Wilfred Pickles, O.B.E.,
Actor and Broadcaster.

This fellow was walking into the doctor's surgery. He bumped into a very young and pretty girl coming out, but she was sighing and sobbing bitterly.
"Oh, come," he said, "it can't be as bad as all that."
She said: "Oh, but it is, the doctor's just told me that I am pregnant."
The man turned to the doctor and said:
"Is it true?"
The doctor said:
"No, but it's cured her hiccups."

Lieut.-General Sir William Pike, K.C.B., C.B.E., D.S.O.,
Chief Commander, St. John Ambulance, 1969-75.

The Brigade Commander was an irascible old man. (But aren't most of them?) His new Brigade Major was straight from the Staff College, and thought he knew all the answers. (But don't most recent graduates from that famous establishment think the same?)
Anyway, the Major was finding his Brigadier difficult to convince on some of his suggested innovations, and was foolish enough to show his irritation at having his bright ideas subjected to a good deal of earthy criticism.
The old man finally exploded.
"I know you think I'm a bloody old fool, but you go next door and you'll find the Staff Captain and he thinks you're a bloody old fool."

Sir Hubert Pitman, O.B.E.,
Sheriff of the City of London, 1959-60.

The head waiter told the commis-waiter:
"Press the 'plat de jour,' it's yesterday's."

The Late Judge M. George Polson, Q.C.,
Recorder of Exeter and Chairman of Isle of Wight Quarter Sessions, 1966-71; Member, General Council of the Bar, 1967-70; Circuit Judge and Honorary Recorder of Exeter, 1972-77.

Some years ago, the late Mr. Justice Cassels was trying a case at Winchester Assizes with a jury. On the second day of the trial, just before the Court adjourned for lunch, one of the jurors got up and said:

"My Lord, could I be excused from attending Court this afternoon as my wife is due to conceive."

The judge replied: "I think you mean that your wife is due to have her baby, don't you? But there," added the judge, "does it matter which of us is right, because in *either* event, it is absolutely vital that *you* should be there."

Winston Churchill used to say that there were only two things more difficult than making an after-dinner speech — one was climbing a wall which is leaning towards you and the other, kissing a girl who is leaning away from you.

Surgeon Rear-Admiral Arnold Ashworth Pomfret, C.B., O.B.E.,
Former Royal Navy Ophthalmic Specialist.

A proposal to erect a statue to an unpopular local dignitary was very much opposed by the town council with one exception.

The argument put forward was, it would afford shelter in bad weather and shade in summer, and the pigeons would undoubtedly express the general feeling in a most appropriate way.

Admiral Sir Reginald Portal, K.C.B., D.S.C.

At a cocktail party a feather-brained young woman was talking a lot of nonsense. After she had uttered some particularly outrageous remark her escort remonstrated:

"Darling — don't you *ever* think before you speak?"

Sweetly she replied:

"How can I think before I've heard what I've got to say."

Sir Hilton Poynton, G.C.M.G.,
Permanent Under-Secretary of State, Colonial Office, 1959-66; Director, Overseas Branch, St. John Ambulance, 1968-75.

A man was just finishing his lunch in a restaurant. The waitress asked if he would take coffee.

"Yes, please," he replied.

The waitress went off but came back quickly and asked:

"With cream or without, sir?"

"Without cream," he replied.

Then followed a much longer wait before the waitress returned, rather flustered, and said apologetically:

"I'm sorry sir. There is no more cream. Will you have it without milk?"

The Rt. Hon. Reg Prentice, J.P., M.P.,
Minister of State Department of Health and Social Security, 1979-81.

This story concerns a large company which required an economic adviser. The managing director decided he needed a well-qualified economist, but it must be someone with only one arm.

A number of candidates were interviewed; many had high qualifications but all were turned down because they had two arms. At last one of them asked him:

"What does it matter? Why do you insist on a one-armed economic adviser?"

"Because I am sick and tired of getting advice which begins 'On the one hand this . . . and on the other hand that . . . '."

J.B. Priestley, O.M., M.A., Litt.D., LL.D., D.Litt., Author.

Two men are sitting up late and have been drinking hard. Their talk, which is about anything, wanders to the weight of babies at birth.

First man: "Ol' man, d'you know that when I was born I only weighed 4½lbs?!"

Second man: "Did you live?"

First man: "Did I live? You ought to see me now!"

Lieutenant-General Sir Steuart Pringle, Bt., Commandant-General, Royal Marines.

All stories, especially after-dinner ones, should be short and to the point. This was well known to at least one small boy, who, on being asked to write a story in class containing elements of Romance, Royalty, Mystery and Religion, completed the task in thirty seconds.

On being asked by the teacher, he read out: "God," said the duchess, "I'm pregnant. 'Oo done it?"

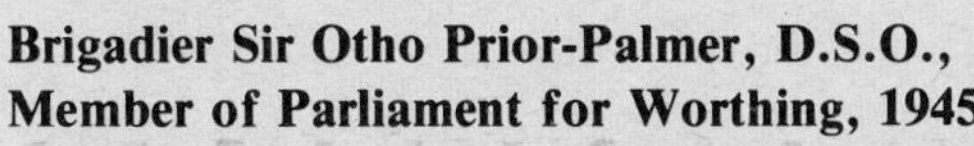

Brigadier Sir Otho Prior-Palmer, D.S.O., Member of Parliament for Worthing, 1945-64.

A speaker said that while changing for dinner his small daughter went into her mother's bathroom and remarked on the size of her tummy.

"Yes, darling, you see daddy has given me a little baby."

After a pause to digest the information the girl rushed into her father's dressing-room:

"Daddy," she cried, "did you give mummy a little baby?"

"Well . . . er . . . yes I did," said father.

"Oh well," said the daughter resignedly, "she's eaten it!"

The Hon. Terence Prittie, M.B.E.,
Author and Journalist; Escaped six times when P.O.W. Germany.

The 11th Duke of St. Albans, with advancing years, decided that he did not like going out to dinner. He preferred his own home.

But there came an occasion when the Duchess bullied him so much that he agreed to go out to dinner — that once. At dinner he sat on his hostess's *left*. As positively the only duke present (and not wanting to be out of his own home anyway), he was annoyed. He decided to go to sleep, and being a man of strong character, he . . . slept.

He slept through the soup, the fish and the joint . . . and awoke with a start. Where was he? At all events, there was a lady, on his right hand, staring fixedly at him.

With old-world courtesy, he turned to her:

"Madam," he said, "I'm afraid I don't know who the devil you are. But at least I can apologise for the filthy food here. We've had to sack the cook."

Dr. Magnus Pyke, O.B.E., F.R.S.C., F.Inst.Biol., F.I.F.S.T., F.R.S.E.,
Scientist and Broadcaster; Chairman of Council, British Association for the Advancement of Science, 1973-77.

During my 25-year sojourn in Scotland I was moved to refer on several occasions to the excise man, for long puzzled to locate an illicit still, who when called upon as a church elder to light the stove one frosty morning in the basement of the church (the church officer being immobilised by rheumatism) suddenly became aware of the reason for his previous inability to identify the work-place of The Queen's competitor for whom he had so long sought.

Even so, however, as he set the stove going in the church basement, he could not forbear to smile at the thought that, while the folks up above were singing hymns, down below the spirit was working.

**Harry Rabinowitz, M.B.E.,
Musical Director, Conductor and Composer.**

Ivan was a very unhappy farmer. His land was on the war-torn Polish/Russian frontier and his citizenship changed constantly from Russian to Polish according to local skirmishes, or national troubles or even international force of arms. This aged him before his time, and he longed for his status to be settled one way or another.

After 50 years of uncertainty a border commission sat; it sat and sat and Ivan grew greyer and more lined. Eventually he heard they'd decided, once and for all. They brought him the news.

Ivan: "Tell me, tell me, what am I finally?"

They: "Ivan, you're to be a Pole."

Ivan: "Thank God. I couldn't have stood another of those Russian winters."

**Steve Race, A.R.A.M.,
Broadcaster and Musician.**

After-dinner speaking is a technique all its own, and one of the most enjoyable moments for me came when someone was giving his "Reply on behalf of the guests."

The scene was an unusually lavish banquet at one of London's dwindling number of multi-star hotels. Commenting on the wonderful fare provided, the speaker pointed out that in 15th century Rome, the Best People were those who were able to observe casually:

"Oh, by the way, I'm dining with the Borgias tonight."

They were naturally proud to be invited he said, as we, the guests, were proud in our turn to be present.

The one difference, however, is that none of those 15th century Top People was ever heard to say:

"Oh, by the way, I dined with the Borgias last night . . . . ."

**The Late Sir Alec Randall, K.C.M.G., O.B.E.,
Diplomat; H.M. Ambassador to Denmark, 1945-52.**

An American had been for some time in a Cornish village, trying to trace his ancestry. He had gone through the parish registers, and when it was time for him to leave he called on the vicar to thank him for all the help he had given to him. He said he wanted to thank him and give him some money for all the trouble he had taken. The vicar said he really didn't want any reward; it had been a pleasure.

"But surely you must have some need in connection with your church," said the American.

The vicar said that it was true that there were expenses in connection with the church, but they were large; the roof, he said, had got the death-watch beetle and must be renewed.

The American asked how much that would be.

The vicar said it was very costly; the expense might amount to be as much as £7,000.

The American said: "Oh, that's about 20,000 dollars. O.K. I'll do it!"

The vicar was overwhelmed with gratitude.

"That," he said, "is most generous. I hardly know how to thank you. When the work is done we shall have a dedication service and we should hope you could come."

The American said it was impossible; he had so much business.

"But," he said, "you could do one thing for me — make a recording of the service and send it to me."

"Very willingly," the vicar said.

The record reached the American and he went into his study to play it, he then burst into the next room raging with anger. His wife asked what was wrong.

"I've been insulted," he said, "they have no gratitude."

She asked just what was wrong, and he said she should come and listen to the play-back.

And so it began:

"Oh, Lord, we thank you for all the blessings you have brought to our church, and above all that wonderful succour (sucker) you sent us from America."

The Late Ted Ray,
Actor and Comedian.

A certain President of the United States was holding a dinner at The White House. Among the guests was a Red Indian Chief dressed in full regalia, even to the Crown and Tail of Feathers.

The President seated his Lady next to the Red Indian Chief, to make him feel at ease and also because the Chief held 51% of a big oil company.

When the dinner commenced and soup was served, the wife of the President smiled at the Chief and said:

"You like-um soupee?"

The Chief acknowledged the remark with a slight nod of the head.

When the second course was served she said:

"You like-um Turkey?"

Again the Chief smiled and nodded. This went on through every course.

After coffee, the Chief was called upon to reply for the guests, which he did in a brilliant speech and in faultless English.

He sat down to a deafening applause, and turning to the President's wife, he said:

"You like-um speechy?"

Lord Reilly,
Director, Design Council, 1960-77; Chief Executive, Crafts Advisory Committee, 1971-77.

Sir Gordon Russell, my predecessor as Director of the Design Council, once found himself at a dinner for a mixed bag of manufacturers and, not knowing his neighbour on his right, asked him what his firm made and got the immediate reply: "Oh, about fifty thousand a year."

In due course I found myself at a similar dinner at Birmingham and, not knowing my neighbour at table, used the same opening gambit and got an even more surprising answer:

"Oh, we make seventeenth century sundial faces."

When I said I didn't believe it, my neighbour replied:

"Oh yes we do — we bury them for a little while and when we dig them up no one can tell the difference."

Sir Eric Richardson, C.B.E., Ph.D., B.Eng., F.P.S., F.R.S.A., Director, The Polytechnic of Central London, 1969-70.

At a conference on linguistics, a professor of Spanish was in conversation with a professor of Irish. The Spanish professor asked if in the Irish language there was the equivalent of the Spanish *mañana.*

After pondering for some moments, the Irish professor said:

"Well, yes we have, indeed we have several, but none of them convey the same sense of urgency."

Sir Ralph Richardson,
Actor; President of the National Youth Theatre and Greater London Arts Association.

There was a man who had the fortune to win a prize on the pools — £1,400 I think it was.

"My goodness, can you believe it?" he asked his wife, "£1,400! Aren't we the luckiest people in the world?"

His wife was not quite as elated as he had expected. Indeed she frowned a little and then said:

"Oh, yes, but what about all the begging letters?"

"Oh, my dear," he replied happily, "you just keep on writing them."

Arnold Ridley,
Author, Playwright, Actor and Producer.

A constable on a late-night beat which took him through a London West End square noticed a well-dressed man leaning drunkenly up against the front door of one of the houses.

"It's all right, officer," said the man, "I live here."

"Then why not go home?" asked the constable.

"Lost my latch key."

"Then why not ring?"

"Have rung."

"Well, there are lights showing. Why not ring again?"
"No. Let 'em wait!"

C.H. Rolph,
Author and Journalist; Director, New Statesman.

The speaker had been droning on for an hour and twenty minutes when he suddenly noticed that a number of his listeners' heads were on the tables.

"I am so terribly sorry," he said.

"Mr. Chairman, I fear I have gone on far too long. I do apologise to everyone. You see, the trouble is I have no watch with me, and there is no clock in the hall."

And a loud voice came from the far end of the hall:

"There's a calendar on the wall behind you."

Sir Ashton Roskill, Q.C., M.A.,
Chairman, Monopolies and Mergers Commission, 1965-75.

Disraeli, when offered the sorbet at a banquet, turning to his neighbour and murmuring appreciatively:

"Thank God, something warm at last."

Lord Ross of Marnock, P.C., M.B.E.,
Secretary of State for Scotland, 1964-70, 1974-76.

The minister, summoned surprisingly to the bedside of the most drunken reprobate in his parish, was even more surprised when he was asked to come closer and offer up a prayer. When he did so the patient sighed and whispered:

"Say it again."

After doing so three times he asked what it was in the prayer that touched him.

The parish drunk replied: "Ah minister, it's no your voice, it's your breath."

Sir Stanley Rous, C.B.E., J.P.,
President, Fédération Internationale de Football Associations, 1961-74.

When I was Secretary of the Football Association I received a letter from an old boy of my student teacher days at Lowestoft.

It started: "I hope you remember me. I remember you very well because you was the best English master what every taught me."

It then went on to ask me for a Cup Final ticket!

The Late Lord Rowallan, K.T., K.B.E., M.C., T.D., D.L.,
Chief Scout, British Commonwealth and Empire, 1945-59; Governor of Tasmania, 1959-63.

At Buckie station during the blackout, there was no station name and no lights, and the Lady Adam was sitting in a compartment opposite an old fishwife. The porter came down the platform shouting:

"Onybody here for Buckie? Onybody here for Buckie?"

At every shout the fishwife winced and drew herself up. As the train steamed out from the platform, the old girl leaned across and with a confidential smile said:

"Ah'm for Buckie mysel' but I wasna going to tell yon speirin' devil."

Lord Rugby,
Farmer.

Indian Chief staying in London hotel after enormous banquet, wakes up in the early hours and says to his wife:

"Squaw — me thirsty, go fetch water."

Off she goes and returns with a glass. Fifteen minutes later — again:

"Squaw, fetch water — me still thirsty."

Dutifully off she trots and brings another glass.

Once more a pause and then yet another demand for water. This time after a long delay she returns empty handed. Angrily he says:

"Squaw — why you no bring water?" Forlornly she replied:

"Master, I wait long time — I look through hole in door — I see big white chief — him sitting on well."

Sir Frederick Russell, C.B.E., D.S.C., D.F.C., F.R.S.,
Marine Biologist, Secretary, Marine Biological Association of the United Kingdom, 1945-65.

A lady was once asked to lunch by a friend. After they had eaten, her host, who was a keen gardener, asked her if she would like him to show her round his garden. She said that she would be delighted.

So he took her round the garden, of which he was very proud, and spoke about the habits of each plant giving at the same time their full Latin names.

When they had finished their perambulation, she thanked him profusely and said:

"What a clever man you are to remember all those Latin names, I only know two."

"Indeed," he replied, "and which are they?"

"One," she said, "is Aurora Borealis, and the other is delirium tremens."

Vice-Admiral Jocelyn Salter, C.B., D.S.O., O.B.E.,
Admiral Superintendent H.M. Dockyard, Portsmouth, 1954-57.

A country vicar was paying a call on an elderly widow whose husband had died some months previously; he was offered a seat in a chair which had an air cushion at the back. He sat down and as he leant back the air cushion burst.

The vicar was naturally embarrassed and was of course eloquent in his apologies — then he saw that the widow was in tears and to his horror she blurted out, through her tears:

"Oh, you couldn't help it, but you see it was my dear husband's last breath."

Mike Sammes,
Recording, Television and Radio Artiste.

The only real drawback was that the previous owners must have been of a somewhat romantic turn of mind, and being enamoured of its delightful appearance, had dubbed it "Fairylands".

Unfortunately, the house was so far out in the wilds on a very open stretch of road with the nearest farm a mile or so down the road that you couldn't very well alter the name or the postman, etc., would never know where the heck you lived!

Anyway, as I said, they'd just got married and were still a bit starry-eyed themselves so they decided to live with it.

All went well, until one cold winter's night they were relaxing round a nice open fire when the front doorbell rang. On opening the door they discovered some friends of theirs had come to call, and with them came bounding a large exuberant young pup. He promptly hurled himself into the dining room and headed full pelt for the fireplace — at which point the cat, dozing peacefully on the hearth-rug, woke up, leapt in one terror-filled bound up the chimney and perched himself on a ledge just out of reach!

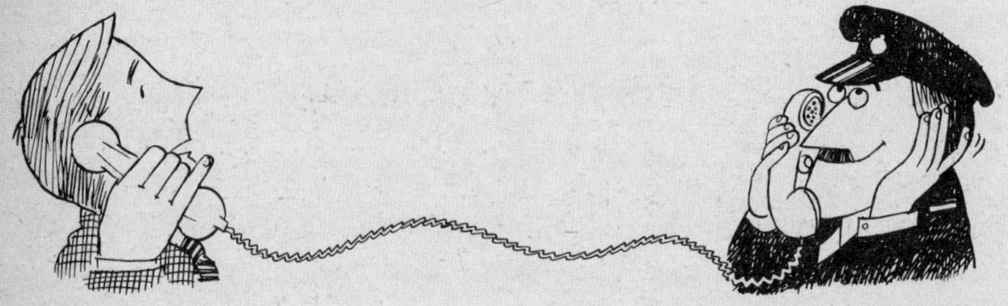

With a blazing fire below, the whole household leapt into action, but to no avail. Resourceful as ever, my friend ran to the hall, picked up the phone and got through to the fire brigade. They answered.

"Hello," he yelled, "is that the fire brigade?"

"Yes, sir, can I help you?"

"Yes, come quickly, there's a cat up the chimney!"

"I beg your pardon, sir?"

"There's a cat up the chimney and we've a roaring fire underneath."

"Oh yes, sir, and where are you speaking from?"

"Fairylands . . . . . . oh! — it's all right, don't bother . . . . he's just come down!"

And I'm sure that to this day they're still quoting the night some idiot rang up to say there was a cat up the chimney in Fairyland, as a prime example of the need for more stringent licensing laws, when in fact it was more in the nature of a narrowly averted cat-astrophe!

Sir Harold Sanders, M.A., Ph.D.,
Chief Scientific Adviser, Ministry of Agriculture, Fisheries and Food, 1955-64.

A detachment of the French Foreign Legion was trudging across the Sahara; they were hot and sticky, dusty and very depressed.

After a long time the commander called them to a halt and addressed them. He said:

"I have two things to tell you. One of them is good news, the other is not so good and that is the one I'll tell you first. We are absolutely and utterly lost and there's nothing to eat but camel dung."

The second in command said: "Very well, mon commandant, now please tell us the good news."

The commander said: "Well, there's plenty of it."

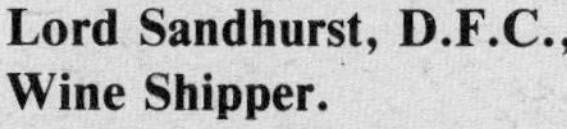

Lord Sandhurst, D.F.C.,
Wine Shipper.

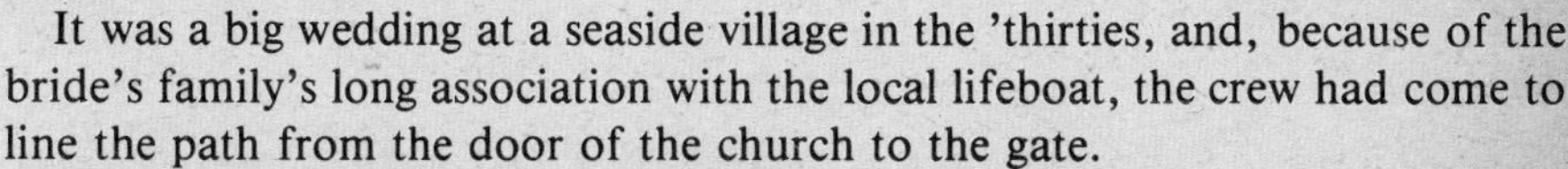

It was a big wedding at a seaside village in the 'thirties, and, because of the bride's family's long association with the local lifeboat, the crew had come to line the path from the door of the church to the gate.

It was still a rowing and sailing lifeboat, so it was a large crew, splendidly arrayed in oilskins, that raised their oars, shining in the sunlight, to make an archway under which the bridal procession passed.

At the front of the watching crowd was a little girl and her mother. They came from the East End of London, and were on holiday.

As always there was a bit of a hush as the bride and groom neared the gate, so the little girl was clearly heard to say:

"Mum, aren't them OARS loverly!"

To which Mum was equally clearly heard to reply:

"'Ush! Them aren't 'Ores, them's bridesmaids."

Sir Donald Sargent, K.B.E., C.B.,
Secretary, National Assistance Board and Supplementary Benefits Commission, 1959-68; Chairman, Civil Service Retirement Fellowship, 1968-74.

A little girl finds her mother with her face covered with face cream and "beauty" preparations, and asks, "What is that for?" and is told:

"That is to make Mummy beautiful."

And she says: "Then why doesn't it?"

Another child, after praying for Mummy and Daddy and various other relations, ends up:

"And, please, God, do look after yourself, because without you we would all be sunk."

A Cambridge don of an older generation has been in the habit of speaking scornfully of some of his younger colleagues whom he fears from time to time are prostituting their vocation by giving talks on the radio.

One day he himself is astonished to receive an invitation to do so, the invitation ending "fee 20 guineas".

The don sends off a telegram accepting, adding:

"Should I send the 20 guineas in advance?"

The Late Sir Jack Scamp,
Director, G.E.C.

A few years ago I took a cricket team to play the staff of the local mental hospital.

When the tea interval arrived I was asked whether I would take my team into the main hall to take tea with the staff and patients instead of following the usual practice of having tea brought to us at the pavilion on the cricket ground.

When we had finished tea I was somewhat surprised when the skipper of the home team rose and made a speech thanking me for bringing my team over to play the hospital staff.

I was asked to reply. I had only spoken two or three sentences when a voice from the back of the hall shouted out:

"Rubbish!"

I carried on speaking, but again the voice shouted:
"Rubbish."

By this time most of the patients, some 100 to 150 were laughing and enjoying themselves enormously, as indeed I fear were some of the staff.

When interrupted for the third time with the shout of "Rubbish", I turned to the superintendent of the hospital, who sat next to me and said:

"What shall I do now, sit down or carry on?"

"Oh, carry on," he said. "We've had this chap in the hospital for about twelve years and this is the first time he has shown signs of having any sense."

Vice-Admiral John Scatchard, C.B., D.S.C., Flag Officer, Second-in-Command, Far East Fleet, 1962-64.

An elderly man complained of a pain in his right leg.

"It's just old age," said the doctor.

"Can't be that," said the patient, "the other leg is the same age, and that don't hurt."

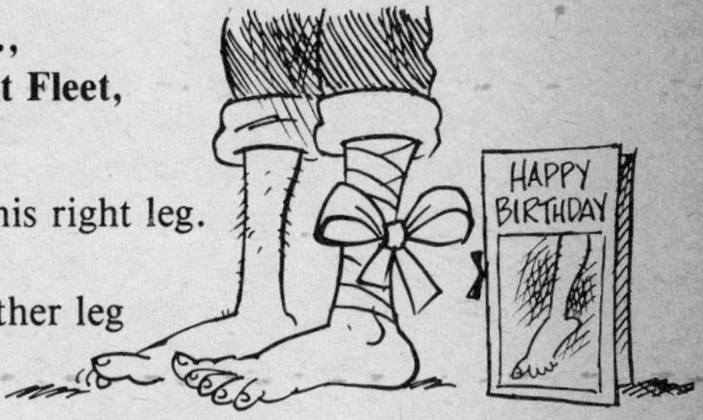

The Late Sir Geoffrey Shakespeare, Bt., Once Secretary to Lloyd George; Ex-M.P. for Norwich; Minister in National Government for many years.

A certain vicar used to boast that he belonged to no political party and no one knew for which party he voted at a General Election. The only possible clue available to anyone was his insistence on choosing the first hymn at a Sunday service after a by-election.

If a Conservative won he would choose the hymn:

"Now thank we all our God."

If a Labour candidate won he would choose the hymn:

"Oh! God our help in ages past."

If a Liberal won he would choose the hymn:

"God moves in a mysterious way, His wonders to perform."

Keith S. Showering,
Chairman and Chief Executive, Allied Breweries Ltd.

There were two Belgians and two Dutchmen who travelled regularly to work on the same train.

After a while it became apparent to the Dutchman that the two Belgians only had one ticket between them and on enquiring how they managed to achieve this, they explained that when the conductor was heard approaching from the other end of the carriage, the two of them left their seats, went into the toilet and locked the door. When the conductor knocked on the door of the toilet saying, "Tickets please", they pushed one ticket under the door, which was duly stamped and pushed back under the door again.

The Dutchmen thought this was a very good idea and the following morning bought one ticket between them, only to find that in their usual carriage there was only one Belgian. They told him what they had done and also told the Belgian that they presumed he must have a ticket as he was travelling on his own.

He said, he did not have a ticket at all and in answer to their enquiry as to how he proposed to manage to travel free of charge, he told them they would have to wait and see until the conductor arrived, but he had no doubt that he would manage it without difficulty.

As soon as the conductor was heard approaching the two Dutchmen immediately went to the toilet and locked the door.

A few moments later the Belgian followed them down the corridor and knocked smartly on the toilet door saying, "Tickets please".

One Dutch ticket appeared under the door.

Lord Simon of Glaisdale, P.C., D.L.,
President, Probate, Divorce and Admiralty Division of the High Court of Justice, 1962-71; a Lord of Appeal, 1971-77.

A man recently went into a veterinary surgery and asked that his dog's tail should be removed. The veterinary surgeon said:

"It is true that that is an operation which we sometimes perform. But it is most unusual on a dog with a beautiful bushy tail like yours. Why do you want it removed?"

The customer replied: "Well, the truth is that my mother-in-law is coming to stay and I do not want there to be the smallest sign of welcome."

General Sir Frank Simpson, G.B.E., K.C.B., D.S.O.,
Commandant, Imperial Defence College, 1952-54; Chief Royal Engineer, 1961-67.

A man due to appear in a minor lawsuit before a subordinate judge met a pal in a pub the night before. After a few pints and much discussion the friend said:

"You'll easily get it settled right. Just send the judge a couple of ducks beforehand."

Next morning the litigant met his solicitor and told him what he intended doing. The solicitor was shocked and said:

"On no account must you do that. We have a pretty weak case anyway, and if you send the judge anything he is bound to rule against you."

When the case came on our friend won.

He took the solicitor over to the pub to celebrate. The solicitor said:

"I am astonished at this result. Frankly, I never thought we had a chance."

The litigant explained that "a couple of ducks" had done it. The solicitor was scandalised:

"Do you really mean to say, after all the warnings I gave you, you sent the judge the ducks?"

"Yes," came the reply, "indeed I did, but I put the other party's name on the label."

The Late Sir Alfred Sims, K.C.B., O.B.E.,
Director-General Ships, Ministry of Defence, 1958-68.

An inexperienced chairman had to propose an important toast before a large assembly of diners.

Eventually the moment approached when he had to brace himself for the task. He was not helped, however, when the red-coated toastmaster approached him and said, with the best of intentions:

"Are you ready now, sir, to speak or shall I let them enjoy themselves a little longer?"

**The Late Rt. Hon. Sir Henry Slesser, Q.C., LL.D.,
H.M. Solicitor-General, 1924; M.P., 1924-29;
Lord Justice of Appeal, 1929-42.**

Lord Hewart, L.C.J., remarked to me at an assembly (where the Ambassadors of the Great Powers were in evening dress) about the representative of a small State:

"The whole Gold Reserve of his country is on his uniform."

The Late Marshal of the Royal Air Force, Sir John Slessor, G.C.B., D.S.O., M.C., Chief of the Air Staff, 1950-52.

In the happy old days, the garrison of Aden always included a battalion of British infantry, of which one company was detached for, I think, six months at a time, and formed the garrison of the island of Kamarin, in the Red Sea.

A fresh battalion had recently taken over at Aden, who were not yet familiar with the tropics and their peculiar diseases. And one day they got a signal from their detached company to say:

"We have a case of beri beri here. What should we do with it?"

Next morning, the reply came from battalion:

"Give it to the Sergeants' Mess. They'll drink anything."

**Barry Granger Smallman, C.M.G., C.V.O.,
Diplomat; British High Commissioner to Bangladesh, 1975-78.**

A small boy, wanting help over a school essay, asked his mother how he came into the world. Unprepared and flustered, she fell back on the stork story, with suitable trimmings.

Looking a little puzzled, he went into the next room and asked grandma how his mother — and for that matter she herself — had arrived.

His grandmother, who had overheard the first exchange, gave him the same reply with even greater circumstantial detail about the sagacity and accuracy of the stork as a delivery agent.

The boy thanked her politely and went off to write his essay. It began:

"So far as I can make out there has not been a natural birth in my family for three generations."

Professor Sir David Smithers, M.D., F.R.C.P., F.R.C.S., F.R.C.R., Professor of Radiotherapy in the University of London, 1943-73.

I have in my time had to do a good deal of after-dinner speaking, mostly to medical audiences. I have told very few stories. I have, however, often tried to work into my theme some appropriate or witty sayings to give it point.

For example, Toscanini once said that he kissed his first woman and smoked his first cigarette on the same day and had never had time for tobacco since.

A notice outside a Temperance meeting said "Alcohol kills slowly", underneath somebody had written "So who's in a hurry."

Sir Edward Maufe, the celebrated architect, arrived late at a banquet. Wending his way round the table he leant over the shoulder of the president to apologise and said in a whisper, "I'm Maufe", to which the president replied, "Oh dear, I'm so sorry you can't stay".

Once explaining why I had never been able to join a political party although both my father and grandfather had been Members of Parliament, I said:

"Political parties seem to me to have too much in common with the airport authority involved in a curious account of a pilot who took his plane on to the runway, ran up the engines not once but three times and then taxied back to base.

"After some delay the plane taxied out again and this time took off without incident. A passenger asked the air hostess what had been wrong and she told him that the pilot had not liked the sound of the engines.

"'So what did they do?' asked the passenger, to which the air hostess replied:

"'They changed the pilot!'."

The Late Sir Lionel Smith-Gordon, Bt., Writer and Translator.

A distinguished Englishman went to New York with the usual letters of introduction.

He was met, on a blazing hot day by a leading citizen who took him to see the sights.

After an exhausting morning they went to the top of the Empire State

Building, and on coming down the host said:

"What can I do for you now?"

Guest: "All I want to have now is something tall and cool and full of gin."

"Easy, man — just come round and meet the wife!"

Air Marshal Sir Frederick Sowrey, K.C.B., C.B.E., A.F.C., U.K. Representative, Permanent Military Deputies Group, C.T.O., 1977-79.

An attractive young girl trying to reach the Far East stowed away on board ship.

After a fortnight or so she was discovered and taken before the captain.

He was surprised to find her well fed and well turned-out and asked who amongst the crew had befriended her. She demurred, but when pressed finally admitted that she had been to the second officer's cabin every day for a bath and a meal.

"And what did he want in return?" was the question.

"I suppose you might say he took advantage of me," was her murmured reply.

"I'll say he did," retorted the captain. "You're on the Liverpool to Birkenhead ferry."

Graham Henry Stainforth, Headmaster of Oundle, 1945-56; Master of Wellington College, 1956-66.

There was once an aged charwoman who was describing to a goggling circle of her cronies her husband's last moments.

"And wot were 'is last words, Mrs. Jones?"
"'E didn't 'ave no last words. Oi was with 'im till *the end*."

**Air Vice-Marshal William P. Stamm, C.B.E., F.R.C.P., F.R.C.Path.,
Senior R.A.F. Consultant in Pathology and Tropical Medicine, 1951-69.**

Two senior retired Army officers were chatting in their club about the short-comings of the modern generation.

"Do you know," said the general, "I was telling my daughter-in-law that my grandfather was killed at Waterloo. She looked up with a sympathetic expression and said: 'Oh, how sad. On what platform did it happen?'"

"Ridiculous," said the brigadier, "as if it mattered what platform he was on."

**Brigadier Sir Alexander Stanier, Bt., D.S.O., M.C., D.L., J.P.,
Lieutenant-Colonel Commanding Welsh Guards, 1945-48.**

An old lady got into a railway carriage where two gentlemen were moaning over their losses at a race meeting. After a time the old lady got up to get out at a station and as she left the carriage she handed one of the gentlemen a £1 note, saying:

"You are obviously so kind to animals I would like to give you this £1."

"We are not particularly kind to animals," replied the gentleman.

"Oh yes, you are," replied the old lady. "I heard you say you put your shirt on that bleeding animal that was scratched."

**The Rt. Hon. David Steel, M.P.,
Leader of the Liberal Party.**

The Archbishop of Canterbury was visiting a small town parish.

The next day in the street a non-churchgoer asked one of the faithful whether his visit had made an impact.

"Well," came the reply, "I would put it this way. At the end of his sermon there was a great awakening in the congregation."

Sir Peter Studd, G.B.E., K.C.V.O.,
Lord Mayor of London, 1970-71.

About noon one day an American couple were passing Runnymede and saw the sign: "Magna Carta signed here 1066".

Wife to husband: "Say, George, what a pity. I guess we just missed it!"

The Late Sir Charles Tennyson, C.M.G.,
Author, Editor and Lawyer; Chairman of Council, Bedford College, University of London, 1946-53.

I remember a middle-aged Whig telling my brother and myself when we were children (round about 1890) that he remembered being taken when about our age to see Lord Palmerston, then Prime Minister, in Downing Street.

Lord Palmerston sat him in a chair on the other side of the table, took a handful of quill pens from the table, and gave them to him with the words:

"Let this be a lesson to you, my boy, always to get what you can out of Her Majesty's Government."

Palmerston was appointed Prime Minister on 5th February, 1855. He retained this office, with one short interval, until he died on 18th October, 1865.

I am now 96 years old.

The Rt. Hon. Jeremy Thorpe,
Leader of the Liberal Party, 1967-76.

Lord William Cecil, Bishop of Exeter, was very vague. The wine was poured out for everyone (save an old lady on his left), who was given water.

"Could I have some wine, my Lord Bishop?"

"Apologies — I thought you were a member of the Temperance League."

"Oh, no — a member of the Purity League."

Bishop: "So sorry — I knew there was something you didn't do!"

Sir Herbert Todd, C.I.E.,
Indian Political Service, 1921-47.

A vet went to a farm to perform artificial insemination of a cow. As he approached the cow he asked the cowman if she was quiet.

"Oh yes," he was answered.

As the vet ran his hand along her back towards the rear, the cow gave him an awful side kick.

"Oh, I thought you said she was quiet."

The old cowman looked puzzled and surprised as he scratched his head. Then light broke over his face.

"Ah," he said, "I guess she ain't seen a bull in a bowler hat afore!"

Sir George Trevelyan, Bt.,
Warden, Shropshire Adult College, 1947-71.

During the Nazi occupation of Norway two friends were sitting in the park in Oslo and a passing Gestapo official overheard one say to the other:

"You know, there's only one man responsible for this horrible war."

The speaker was at once arrested and marched off to police headquarters. Here he was asked to repeat his remark.

"Certainly," says he, "I said that there was only one man responsible for this horrible war."

"And who is that man?"

"Why, Winston Churchill, of course."

The interrogator, somewhat taken aback, said:

"Yes, um, yes, of course, and you are right. You may take your hat and go."

At the door the Norwegian turned, paused and looked back and asked:

"By the way, who did you think it was?"

The Late Air Vice-Marshal Stanley Vincent, C.B., D.F.C., A.F.C., D.L., Air Officer Commanding No. 11 Group, Royal Air Force, 1948-50.

A fat man went to his doctor to see if he could do anything about his obesity. He was given pills to be taken every night for two months with a promise of a loss of two stone.

The first night he took the pill and dreamed the most marvellous dream, being on a beautiful island, inhabited by the most gorgeous girls — all naked — who he proceeded to chase round the island. The result was a pound gone in the morning.

This happened every night for two months and the two stone was dutifully lost.

Another man, equally fat, asked him how he had done it. Off he went to the same doctor for the same prescription — but his dreams were of a rocky island on which *he* was chased every night by horrible creatures, but the result was the same — two stone lost.

He went to the doctor to ask why he had such horrible dreams and the first man such good ones. The doctor's reply was:

"Oh well, you see, he was a private patient!"

Lord Wallace of Campsie, K.St.J., J.P., D.L., Industrialist; Past-President, Glasgow Chamber of Commerce.

Patrick from Dublin was crossing St. Peter's Square on a wet and gusty evening, his collar turned up against the wind. Suddenly, he clutched at his chest and collapsed in a puddle on the ground.

Providentially, friends were close at hand and immediately rushed to his aid.

"Quick," said Patrick, "get me a rabbi."

"But, Patrick, you're a good Catholic."

"Ah sure, sure," was the reply, "but I wouldn't dream of bringing His Holiness out on a night like this!"

Ian Wallace, Opera Singer, Actor and Broadcaster.

In those far off days when it was possible to get into Oxford or Cambridge University with the minimum of academic qualifications, provided the candidate was a first-class athlete, a serious situation arose at one of these universities — I'm not certain which — one year. The best player in the Rugby XV had not done a stroke of work and had scored such poor marks in his examinations that there seemed no alternative but to send him down a year early — thereby ensuring dire consequences on the field of play.

The young man was supposed to be reading history, and it was known that the chairman of the board of examiners in this subject was an old Rugby blue with his heart definitely in the right place. Discreet pressure on him was brought to bear by various interested parties. He finally agreed that the sporting honour of the university was at stake, and that some concession would have to be made.

He decided that he would set this master of the line-out and set scrum a simple paper which required him to answer only one question. A correct answer would secure a year's reprieve.

"It will be a really simple question?" insisted the leader of the deputation, "He's not very bright."

"You have nothing to worry about," smiled the chief examiner.

Our husky friend entered the room warily, as if there were a danger of conceding a penalty before kick-off. The invigilator handed him the paper, and, as he read the question, a frown appeared on his scarred brow and he nervously pinched his broken nose. The words that caused this agitation were:

"Tell in your own words the best known story about Queen Elizabeth and Sir Walter Raleigh."

For a few minutes he sat, head in hands, and it seemed to the silently watching invigilator that defeat in the Varsity Match had become a melancholy foregone conclusion.

Then he straightened up and smiled, revealing the gap where two front teeth should have been, indeed were, before a collision with a 16-stone Harlequin had wrenched them from their sockets the Saturday before last. He seized his pen and began to write.

"One day Queen Elizabeth was riding through the streets of Coventry stark naked on a big white horse. By a strange coincidence Sir Walter Raleigh was visiting an aunt in the city that day. When he saw the Queen, he dashed forward and ripped off his cloak, saying, 'Honi soit qui mal y pense!' That means 'Madam, take my cloak. Thy need is greater than mine'. To which she replied, 'Dieu et mon droit!', which, of course, means, 'My God, you're right!'."

Judge Martyn Ward,
A Circuit Judge, since 1972.

A secretary agreed to work late with her boss and when they had finished work offered to drop him off at his home in her car.

On the way he offered to buy her a meal, which she accepted. They also had a couple of bottles of wine and quite spontaneously, for they were not having an affair, ended up in her flat and in bed. Time passed quickly and too late they realised that his wife would need, for that hour, an extremely good explanation for his lateness.

He asked his secretary for, and got, a piece of chalk. Arriving home, his irate wife was waiting.

"And where do you think you've been?"

"Well, actually," he replied, "I was working late with my secretary, I took her for a meal, one thing led to another and we ended up in bed in her flat."

The wife screamed: "You liar. You've been playing darts with the boys. You've still got the piece of chalk behind your ear."

Lord Wigg, P.C.,
President, Betting Office Licensees' Association.

There was a member of the House of Lords who suspected that a trainer had been doping. So, for months, whenever the trainer had a runner, his lordship was there watching every movement. There came a day when the trainer had a filly which was not much fancied and, after he saddled her, his lordship noticed the trainer take a little box from his pocket, take something out, and gave it to the filly, to swallow. His lordship pounced.

"What's that?"

"Oh, my lord," said the trainer, "it's just a little sweetmeat —nothing at all. I'll have one and you have one."

The trainer swallowed the tablet and his lordship found himself doing the same.

A few moments later the jockey came into the ring and the trainer said:

"Take her down very quietly, jump her off, lie on the rails — about fourth — and when you come to the straight, pull her out and go on and win. If anything passes you it will either be his lordship or me."

Lord Williamson, C.B.E., J.P.,
General Secretary, National Union of General and Municipal Workers, 1946-61.

After a very happy and successful meeting, the secretary asked the chief speaker:

"What are your expenses?"

"Nothing," the speaker answered.

"Are you quite sure?" asked the secretary.

"Certain," said the speaker. "I have no expenses."

"Thank you very much," said the secretary. "We have a number of gentlemen who kindly refuse to accept any expenses, and the money we save we put into a special fund so that we will be able to afford to invite better speakers in the future."

Lord Willis, F.R.S.A.,
Film, Radio and T.V. Playwright.

Some years ago, when I was doing some research for a film about London, I worked, among other things, as a barrow-boy in the Rupert Street market off Shaftesbury Avenue.

One day I was setting up the stall with Fred, the

owner, when two nuns came through the market carrying shopping bags. Fred dropped everything, rushed out to greet them and gave the first of the nuns a very passionate and familiar kiss.

When he returned I remonstrated with him, pointing out that though I am not a particularly religious person, this was just not the sort of thing that you did with nuns, to which he replied with a smile:

"Oh, don't worry, mate, they are from 'The Sound of Music' up at the Palace Theatre."

Lord Wolfenden, C.B.E.,
President, Chelsea College, University of London.

I had a case of whisky in my cellar and my wife told me to empty each and every bottle down the sink, or else . . . . so I reluctantly proceeded with the unhappy task.

I drew the cork from the first bottle and poured the contents down the sink, with the exception of one glass, which I drank.

I pulled the cork from the second bottle and did likewise, with the exception of one glass, which I drank.

I emptied the third bottle, except for a glass, which I drank and then I took the cork from the fourth sink, poured the glass down the bottle and drank that too.

I pulled the bottle from the next glass, drank one sink out of it, and emptied the rest down the cork.

Then I pulled the sink from the next bottle and poured it down the glass and drank the cork, and finally I took the glass from the last bottle, emptied the cork, poured the sink down the rest and drank the pour.

When I had everything emptied, I steadied the house with one hand, counted the bottles and glasses and corks with the other and found there were 29.

To make sure, I recounted them when they came by again and this time there were 74.

As the house came around the next time I counted them again, and finally I had all the houses and sinks and glasses and cork and bottles counted, except one house, which I then drank.

Lord Holderness, P.C., D.L.,
Minister for Overseas Development, 1970-74.

My appeal for advice to my father, Lord Halifax, when I first began speaking in public was met thus:

He told me he had himself, many years earlier, made a similar appeal to a great orator of the day, who had replied:

"Speak as long and as often as you can; and you will soon acquire that natural contempt for your audience which every bore instinctively has."

The Late Rt. Hon. Arthur Woodburn, D.Litt.,
Politician and Writer; Member of Parliament for Clackmannan, 1939-70.

The Scots are reputed to be mean. This is a mistake. They are only careful and hate waste.

An illustration of this is the story of a tourist in a train in the Highlands discovering he wanted to smoke, turning to the Scot who was the other passenger to ask if he could have a match.

"Oh certainly," said the Scot, carefully taking one match out of his box.

But when the tourist discovered that he had forgotten his cigarettes and dolefully confessed his trouble to the Scot, the latter thereupon extended his hand to the tourist saying:

"Well, you'll no' be needing the match."

The Late Rt. Hon. George Woodcock, C.B.E.,
General Secretary, Trades Union Congress, 1960-69.

Some years ago, when I was a weaver, a fellow work-mate asked me if I proposed to go to the wedding of a mutual friend.

"No," I said, "I haven't been invited."

"Well," he said, "neither have I, but I haven't been told to stay away."

Air Marshal Sir Peter Wykeham, K.C.B., D.S.O., O.B.E., D.F.C., A.F.C.,
Deputy Chief of the Air Staff, 1967-69.

A professor of Yale University was an after-dinner speaker at an academic banquet in England.

"As you know," he began, "I come from Yale, and I want to frame my speech around those four letters." His listeners looked hopeful.

"Y," said he, "stands for Youth: our society is a young one. . . " and he talked about Youth for fifteen minutes.

"Now A," he said, "is for Ambition, the great American virtue . . . ." The guests settled down as he spoke for twenty minutes on Ambition.

"L stands for Learning," he declaimed; and gave fifteen more minutes to Learning.

"And E for that great institution, Education . . . . ." His listeners now low in their chairs, he wound up with twenty minutes on Education. As he sat down, he eagerly asked his neighbour, whose eyes were glazing over: "How did I do?"

"We enjoyed it very much," was the faint reply, "and we're all so glad that you're not from Massachusetts Institute of Technology."

The Rt. Hon. Lord Wylie, V.R.D.,
Advocate; Senator of the College of Justice in Scotland.

We live in an age in which we are deluged by statistics. The trouble about statistics however is that they can be used to prove practically anything at all, and in the last analysis they mean so little.

Every time I see a set of statistics produced to support a particular proposition I always recall a definition I once heard of a statistician.

He is a person who can lie with his head in the ice box and his feet in the oven and be able to say that, on the whole, he was feeling quite normal.

Over six hundred contributors sent stories to Oxfam for this book. Unfortunately, through lack of space, we have not been able to include all the stories received. In addition, several stories were received from different sources: in this case, the published version is the one received first.

The publishers and the Directors of Oxfam gratefully acknowledge all these contributions below.

Nigel J. Abercrombie
The Marquess of Aberdeen and Temair
Gerald Abraham, CBE
The Late Gerald Abrahams
Ronald Adam, OBE
Air Commodore Cyril D. Adams, CB, OBE
Sir Campbell Adamson
Sir William Addison
Robert J. Adley, MP
Paul Adorian
The Late John E. Aiken, CB
Brian Aldiss
Reginald J. Allerton, CBE
The Rt. Hon. Julian Amery, MP
General Sir John Anderson, GBE, KCB, DSO
Walter C. Anderson, CBE
Earl Annesley
Lord Ardwick
The Duke of Argyll
John H. Arkell, CBE
The Late Rear-Admiral Reginald W. Armytage, GC, CBE
Sir Ove Arup, CBE
The Late Lord Arwyn
Gilbert Ashton, MC
Rear-Admiral Ian G. Aylen, CB, OBE, DSC
The Late Sir Felix Aylmer, OBE (Sir Felix Aylmer-Jones)

Lieut.-Colonel Henry H. Barneby, TD
Sir Charles Bateman, KCMG, MC
Sir Darrell Bates, CMG, CVO
The Marquess of Bath
The Late Sir Harry Batterbee, GCMG, KCVO
The Late Sir Leonard Behrens, CBE
Geoffrey F. Bell, MC
Walter Bell, CMG
The Late Sir Thomas Bennett, KBE
Sir Eric Berthoud, KCMG
John Biggs-Davison, MP
H.A. Roy Binney, CB
Derek Birch
Major-General Sir Alec Bishop, KCMG, CB, CVO, OBE
Professor George Bond, FRS
The Rt. Hon. Arthur Bottomley, OBE, MP
Professor Sir Robert Bradlaw, CBE
Lord Brockway
Ninian Brodie of Brodie
Robert N. Bruce, CBE, TD

Rear-Admiral Benjamin Bryant, CB, DSO, DSC
Rear Admiral Sir Kenneth Buckley, KBE
The Late Sir Alan Burns, GCMG, KSt.J

Nigel Calder
Alan C. Campbell-Orde, CBE, AFC
The Earl of Carnarvon
Lord Carrington, KCMG, PC, MC
Air Commodore John Cecil-Wright, AFC, TD
Air Vice-Marshal Sir Bernard Chacksfield, KBE, CB
Frank Chacksfield
Sir Ross Chesterman
Sir Fife Clark, CBE
Leonard Clark, OBE
Michael W. Clark, CBE
William G. Clark, MP
Denzil R.N. Clarke
Thomas E.B. Clarke, OBE
Sir Alec Clegg
Walter Clegg, MP
Lord Cochrane of Cults
Professor John M. Cocking
The Late Sir Laurence Collier, KCMG
Lord Collison, CBE
The Late Deryck V. Cooke
Henry Cooper, OBE
The Late Sir Conrad Corfield, KCIE, CSI, MC
Alan G.W. Coulthard
Lord Craigton, PC, CBE
Professor Bernard Crick
Andrew Cruickshank, MBE
The Late Sir Duncan Cumming, KBE, CB

Sir Leonard Daldry, KBE
John B. da Silva, CMG
The Late Major-General Edward de Fonblanque, CB, CBE, DSO
Sir Arthur de la Mare, KCMG, KCVO
Fred Desmond
Sir Maurice Dorman, GCMG, GCVO
The Late Lord Douglas of Barloch, KCMG
Professor A.N. Duckham, CBE
Professor Alec N. Duckworth, CBE
Clive Dunn
The Most Rev. George P. Dwyer, Archbishop of Birmingham (RC)

Sir George Edwards, OM, CBE, FRS
The Late The Very Rev. Vorley S. Ellis
Air Marshal Sir Aubrey Ellwood, KCB, DSC
Lieut.-General Sir John Evetts, CB, CBE, MC
Professor Hans J. Eysenck

Lord Forbes, KBE
Francis Ford-Robertson, OBE
The Late Earl Fortescue, MC, TD
Admiral of the Fleet, Lord Fraser of North Cape, GCB, KBE
The Rt. Hon. Thomas Fraser

Vice-Admiral Sir Donald Gibson, KCB, DSC
Sir Alexander Giles, KBE, CMG
Sir Leslie Glass, KCMG
Judge Francis Glazebrook
The Late Sir Louis Gluckstein, GBE, TD, QC
Sir William Gorell Barnes, KCMG, CB
Judge Brian Grant

The Late Sir Alexander Grantham, GCMG
Air Vice-Marshal John A. Gray, CB, CBE, DFC, GM
Professor Thomas C. Gray, CBE
The Late Lieut.-General Sir Wyndham Green, KBE, CB, DSO, MC
Lord Greville
The Late Sir Eric Griffith-Jones, KBE, CMG, QC
Air Marshal Sir Victor Groom, KCVO, KBE, CB, DFC

Norman Hackforth
The Earl of Halsbury, FRS
Sir Robert Hardingham, CMG, OBE
Sir Ronald Harris, KCVO, CB
Major-General Desmond Harrison, CB, DSO
The Late Sir Harwood Harrison, Bt, TD
Benjamin J. Hartwell, OBE
The Late Frank Harvey
Lord Harvington, PC
The Late Sir Michael Hawkins, KCVO, MBE
Sir Nicholas Henderson, GCMG
The Marquess of Hertford
General Sir Reginald Hewetson, GCB, CBE, DSO
Lord Hinton of Bankside, OM, KBE, FRS
The Late Sir Alan Hitchman, KCB
The Late Colonel Sir Claude Holbrook, CBE
Major-General Sir Noël Holmes, KBE, CB, MC
Frank R. Hornby, CBE
Major-General David R. Horsfield, OBE
Dr. Eric W. Horton
Sir Benedict Hoskyns, Bt
Rear-Admiral Peter N. Howes, CB, DSC
Professor Robert A. Humphreys, OBE
The Late Michael H. Huxley

Christopher Ironside, OBE
The Late Rt. Hon. George Isaacs
Robert Ives

Air Vice-Marshal Sir Ralph Jackson, KBE, CB
John R.M. Jacobs
Sir Harold Jeffreys, FRS
Julian Jeffs, QC
John G. Jenkins, CBE
John Joel
The Late F. Stephen Joelson
Professor Ronald C. Johnston
Professor Emrys Jones
Air Marshal Sir Richard Jordan, KCB, DFC
Michael Joughin, CBE

Kaplan Kaye
Professor Bryan Keith-Lucas
David B. Kelly
Sir Harold Kent, GCB, QC
The Hon. Sir Michael Kerr, QC
The Late Sir Charles Key, KBE, CB
The Late Sir Geoffrey King, KCB, KBE, MC
Esmond Knight
David Kossoff

Lord Langford, OBE
Admiral Sir Horace Law, GCB, OBE, DSC

Lord Lee of Newton, PC
Lord Leighton of St. Mellons
The Late Brigadier Herbert W. Le Patourel, VC
The Earl of Limerick
Sir Trevor Lloyd-Hughes
Sir Ben Lockspeiser, KCB, FRS
The Late Brigadier Stephen H. Longrigg, OBE
Sir Niall Lynch-Robinson, Bt, DSC

The Late Donald McCullough
Major-General Hugh Macdonald-Smith, CB
The Rt. Hon. Basil McIvor
The Late John Mackie, OBE, MP
Professor Robert H. Macmillan
The Late Sir George McRobert, CIE
The Late Sir Lance Mallalieu, QC
The Earl of Malmesbury, TD, KSt.J
Wolf Mankowitz
Sir Hugo Marshall, KBE, CMG
Sir Geoffrey Meade, KBE, CMG, CVO
Sir John Mellor, Bt
Sir Robert Milnes Coates, Bt, DSO
Sir Anthony Milward, CBE
Lieut.-Colonel Brian G.B. Mitchell, DSC
Sir William Montagu-Pollock, KCMG
Professor William I.C. Morris
Air Vice-Marshal Roger Mortimer, CBE
Professor W.E. Morton
Sir William Mount, Bt

Sir Joseph Napier, Bt, OBE
Sir Charles Newbold, KBE, CMG, QC
Sir John Newson-Smith, Bt
Vice-Admiral Sir Geoffrey Norman, KCVO, CB, CBE

Sir Harry Page
The Late Sir John Patterson, KBE, CMG
Cornelius J. Pelly, CMG, OBE
Major Sir William Pennington-Ramsden, Bt
The Late Sir James Penny, KCIE, CSI
Air Vice-Marshal Allan Perry-Keene, CB, OBE
Professor Calbert I. Phillips
The Late Brigadier Sir Robert Pigot, Bt, DSO, MC
Sir Roy Pinsent, Bt
Sir George Pollock, QC
Sir Fred Pritchard, MBE
Sir Dennis Proctor, KCB

The Late Sir Lincoln Ralphs
The Hon. Sir Peter Ramsbotham, GCMG, GCVO
The Rt. Hon. James Ramsden
Sir Herbert Redfearn
Sir Norman Reid
Sir John Richmond, KCMG
Malcolm L. Rifkind, MP
The Rev. Canon Nicholas Rivett-Carnac, Bt
Brian Rix, CBE
Sir Frank Roberts, GCMG, GCVO
The Late Sir Howard Roberts, CBE
The Late Colonel Sir Thomas Roberts, Bt, CBE
Sir Kenneth Roberts-Wray, GCMG, QC
The Late Major-General Cecil B. Robertson, CB, CBE, MC
Sir John Rodgers, Bt
Earl Russell
Sir Archibald Russell, CBE, FRS

Judge John C. Rutter

Viscount Sandon, TD
Vice-Admiral Sir Guy Sayer, KBE, CB, DSC
The Late Viscount Scarsdale, TD
The Late Sir Frederick Scopes
Sir David Scott-Fox, KCMG
Air Vice-Marshal David Scott-Malden, DSO, DFC
Admiral Sir Alan Scott-Moncrieff, KCB, CBE, DSO
Professor Judah B. Segal, MC
The Earl of Selborne
Lord Sherfield, GCB, GCMG
Sir Graham Shillington, CBE
The Rt. Hon. Dr. Robert Simpson
Vice-Admiral Sir Richard Smeeton, KCB, MBE
Sir Ralph Smith-Marriott, Bt
Brigadier The Rt. Hon. Sir John Smyth, Bt, VC, MC
Sir Michael Sobell
Sir Rupert Speir
Sir Cecil Stafford-King-Harman, Bt
Lord Stanley of Alderley
Sir Robert Stanley, KBE, CMG
Tom Stoppard, CBE, FRSL
Lord Strange
Lord Strauss, PC
Sir James Stubblefield, FRS
Sir William Swallow
E.W. Swanton, OBE
The Late Sir Cecil Syers, KCMG, CVO
Air Vice-Marshal William Sykes, OBE

Kenneth Tallerman, MC
Lord Taylor of Gryfe, FRSE
Lord Taylor of Mansfield, CBE
Lieut.-General Sir Allan Taylor, KBE, MC
Sir Peter Tennant, CMG, OBE
Sir Herbert Thompson, CIE
The Late Major-General Sir Treffry Thompson, KCSI, CB, CBE
The Late Colonel Sir Colin Thornton-Kemsley, OBE, TD
Professor William H. Thorpe, FRS
The Late Sir Michael Turner, CBE

Lord Vaizey of Greenwich

Lord Wakefield of Kendal
Sir James Walker, Bt
The Rt. Hon. Sir Derek Walker-Smith, Bt, QC, MP
The Late Sir Geoffrey Wallinger, GBE, KCMG
Lord Walston, CVO
Judge Sir Raymond Walton
Air Chief Marshal Sir Neil Wheeler, GCB, CBE, DSO, DFC, AFC
Professor Peter Willmott
Viscount Wimborne

INDEX